THIS BOOK BELONGS TO:

COLOR CHARTS TEST

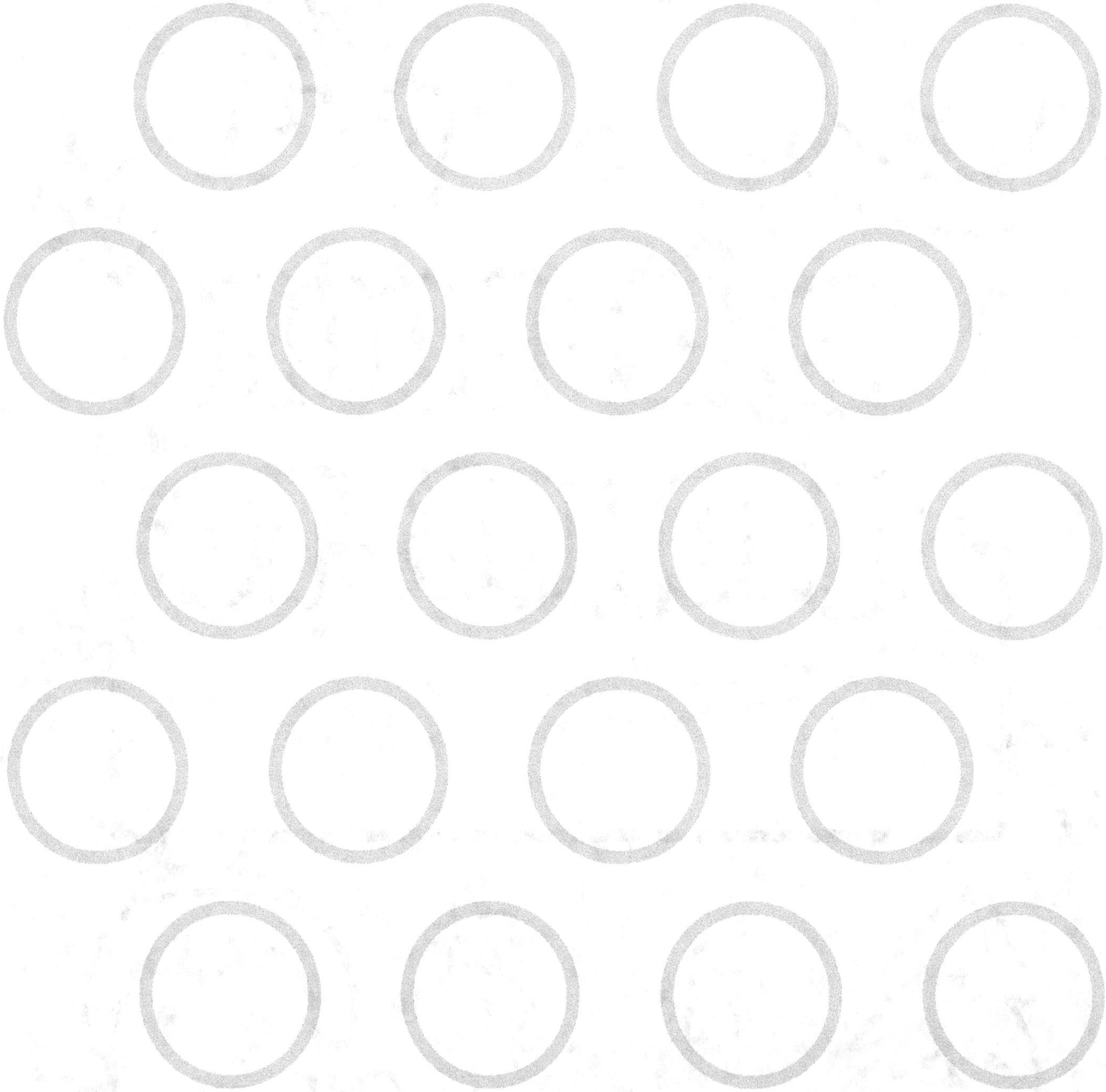

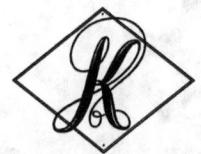

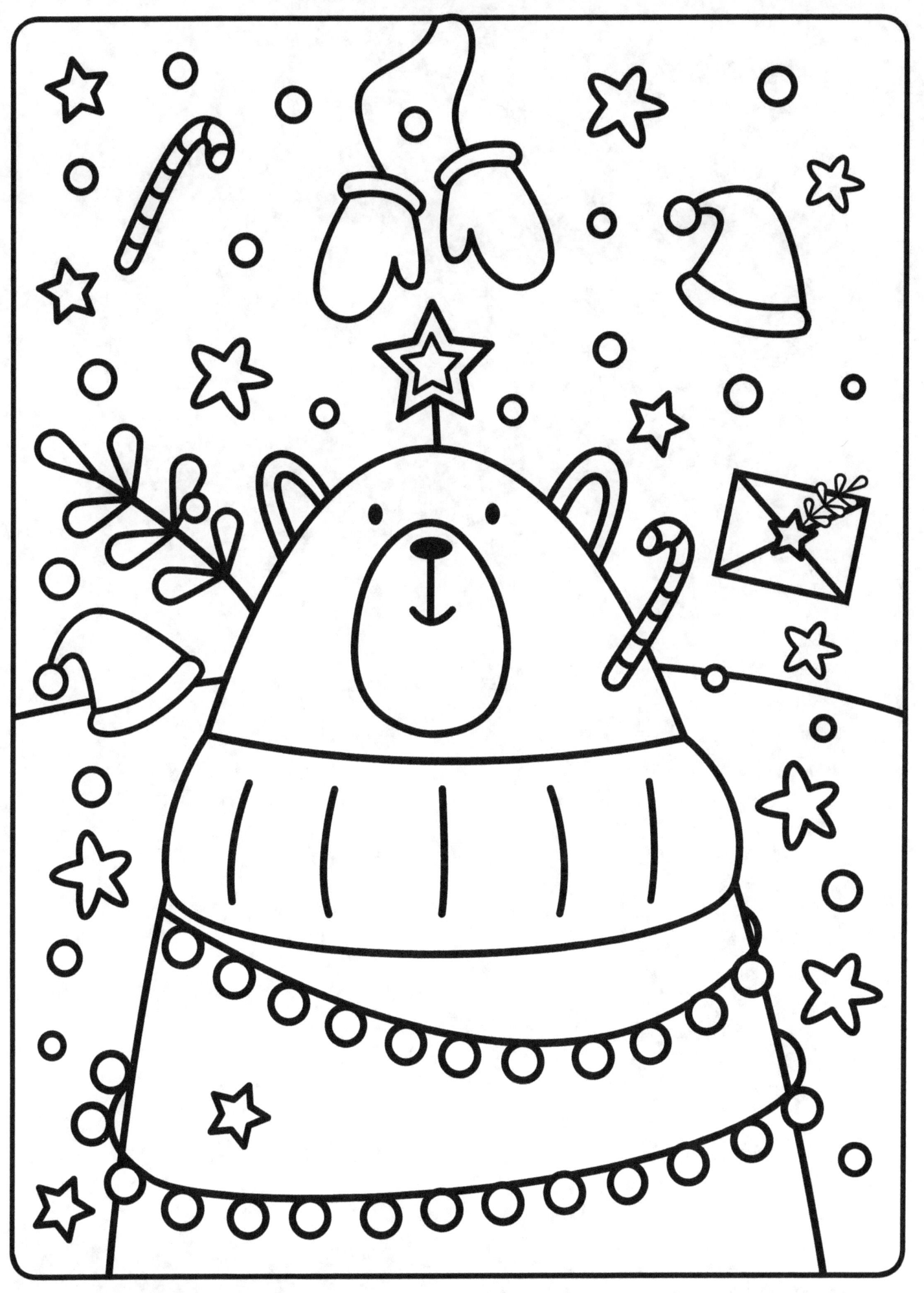

COLOR CHARTS TEST

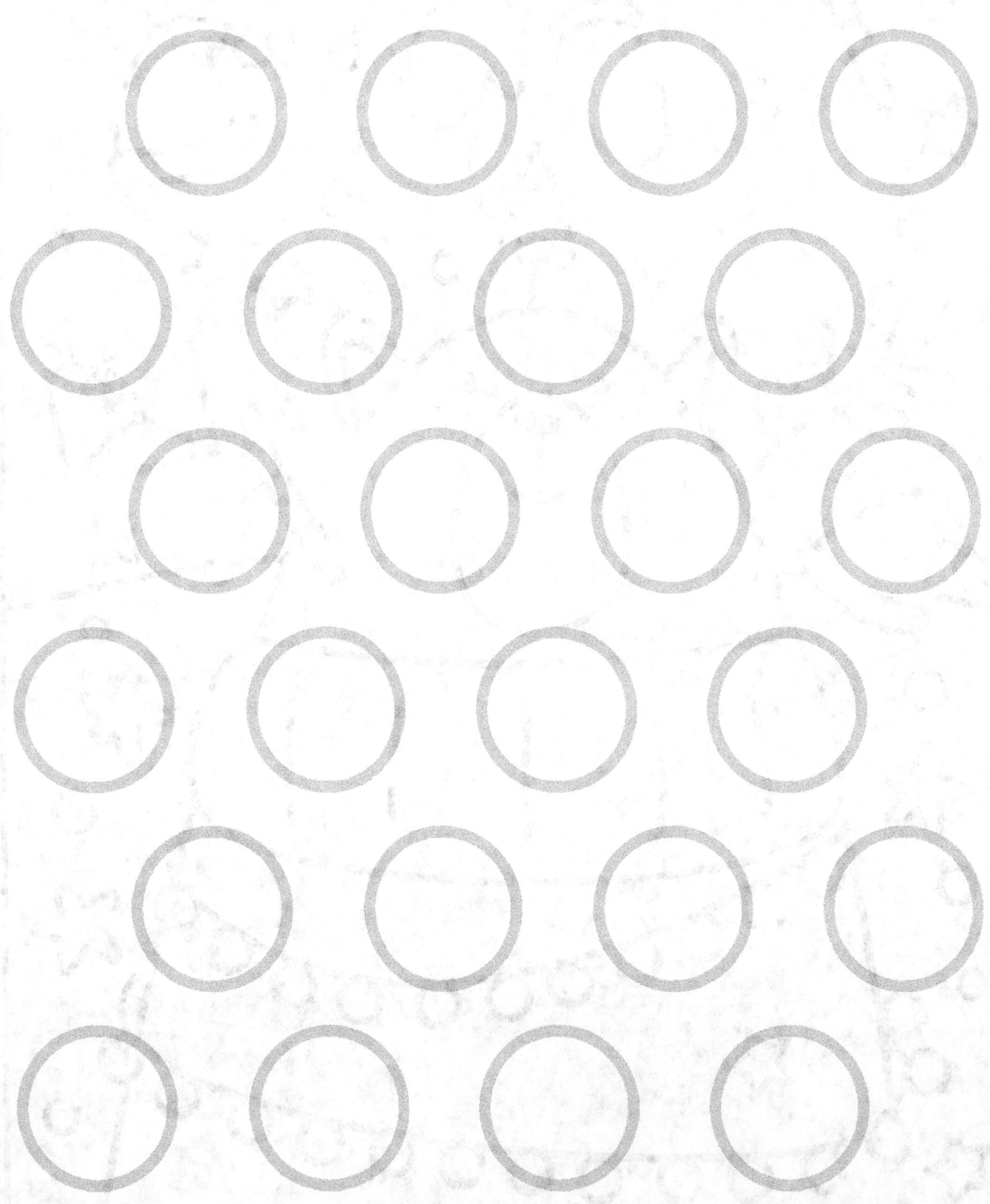

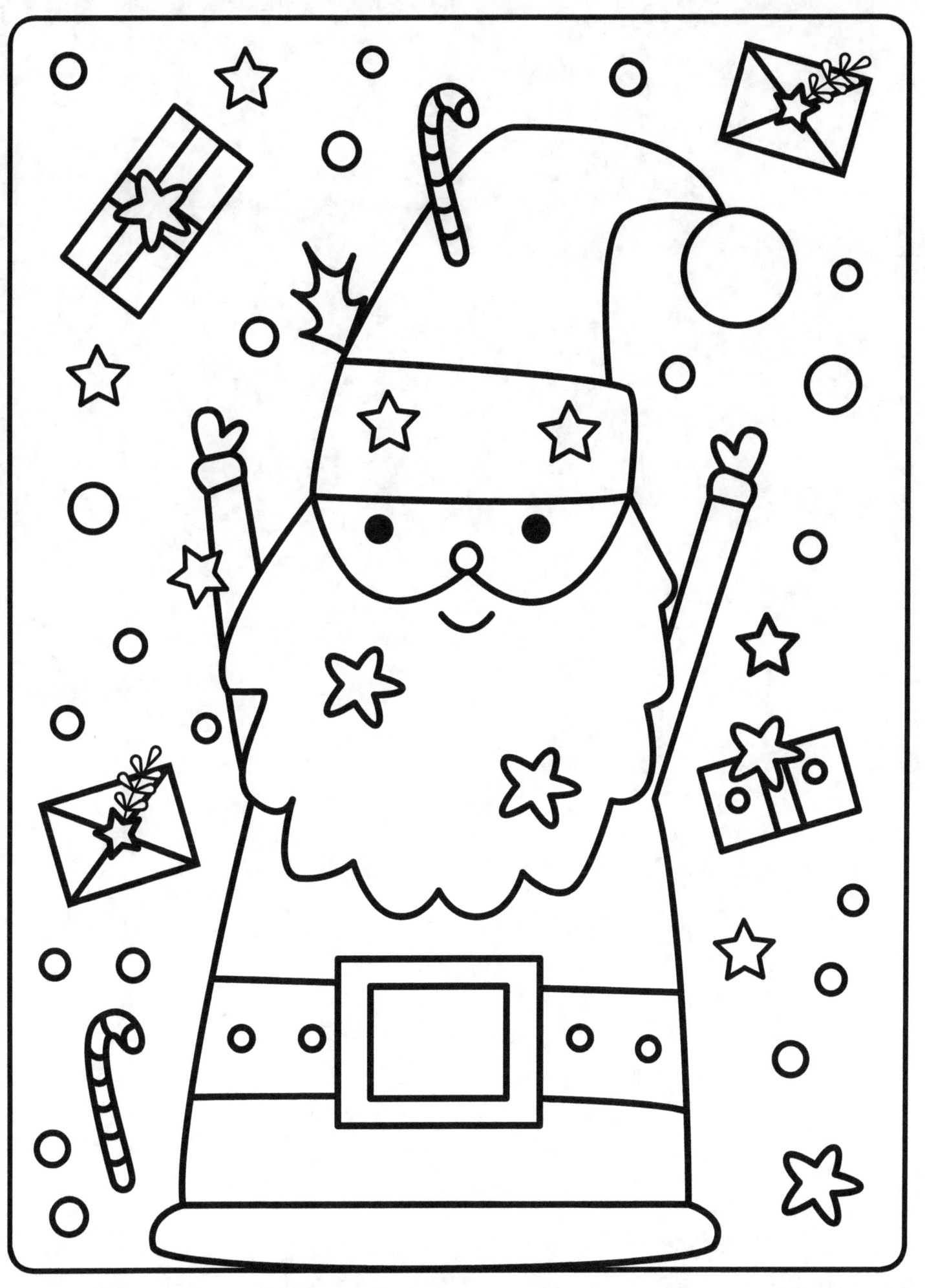

COLOR CHARTS TEST

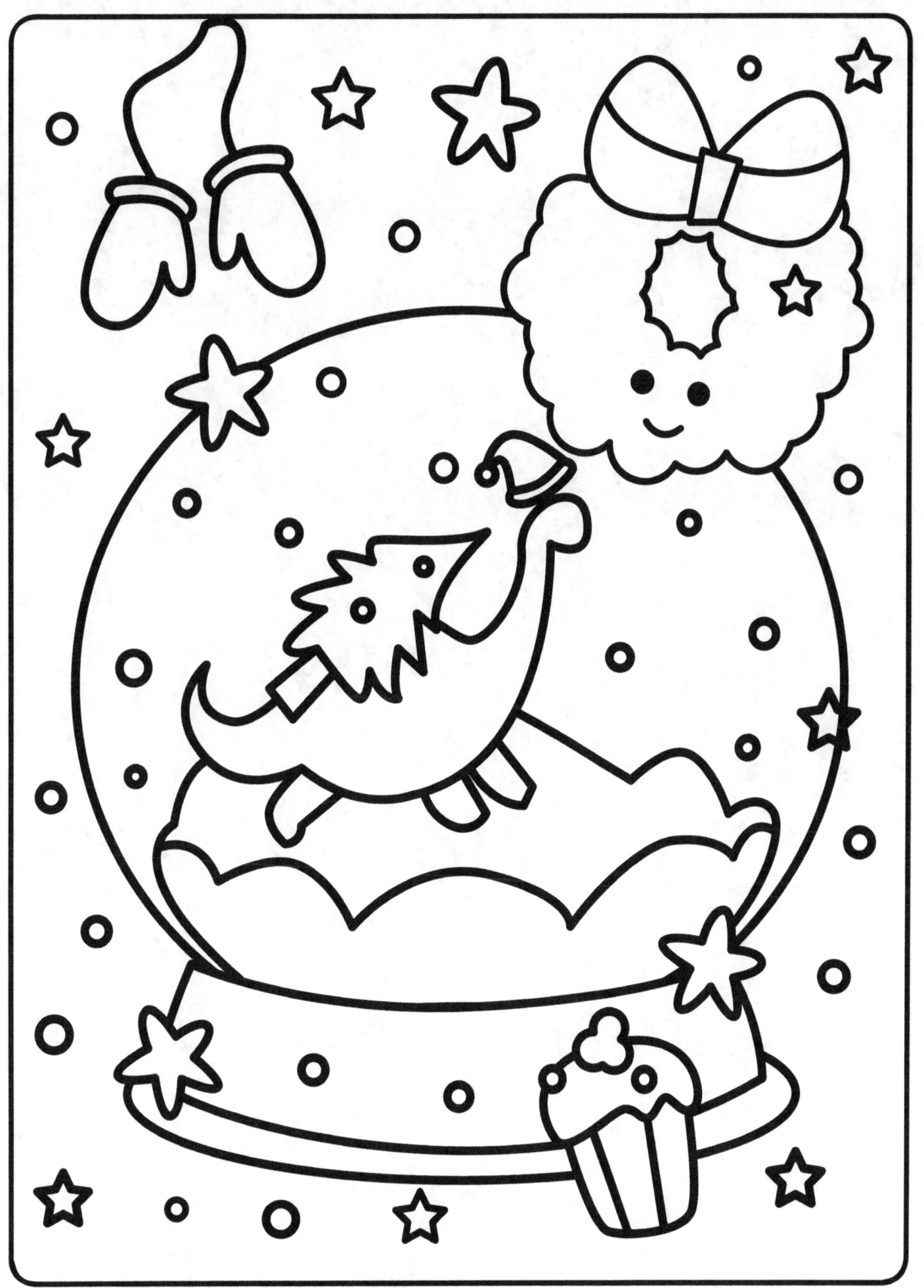

COLOR CHARTS TEST

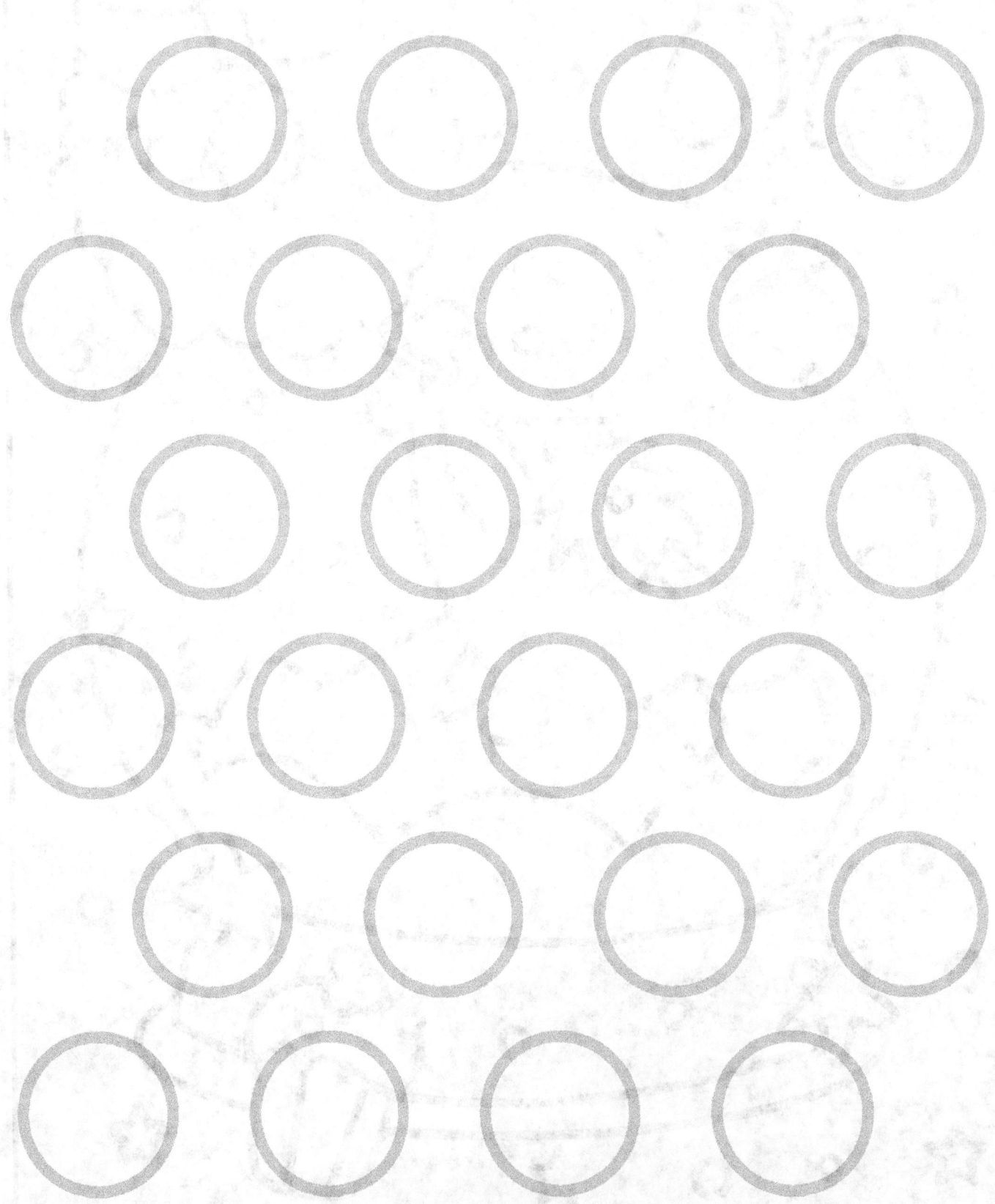

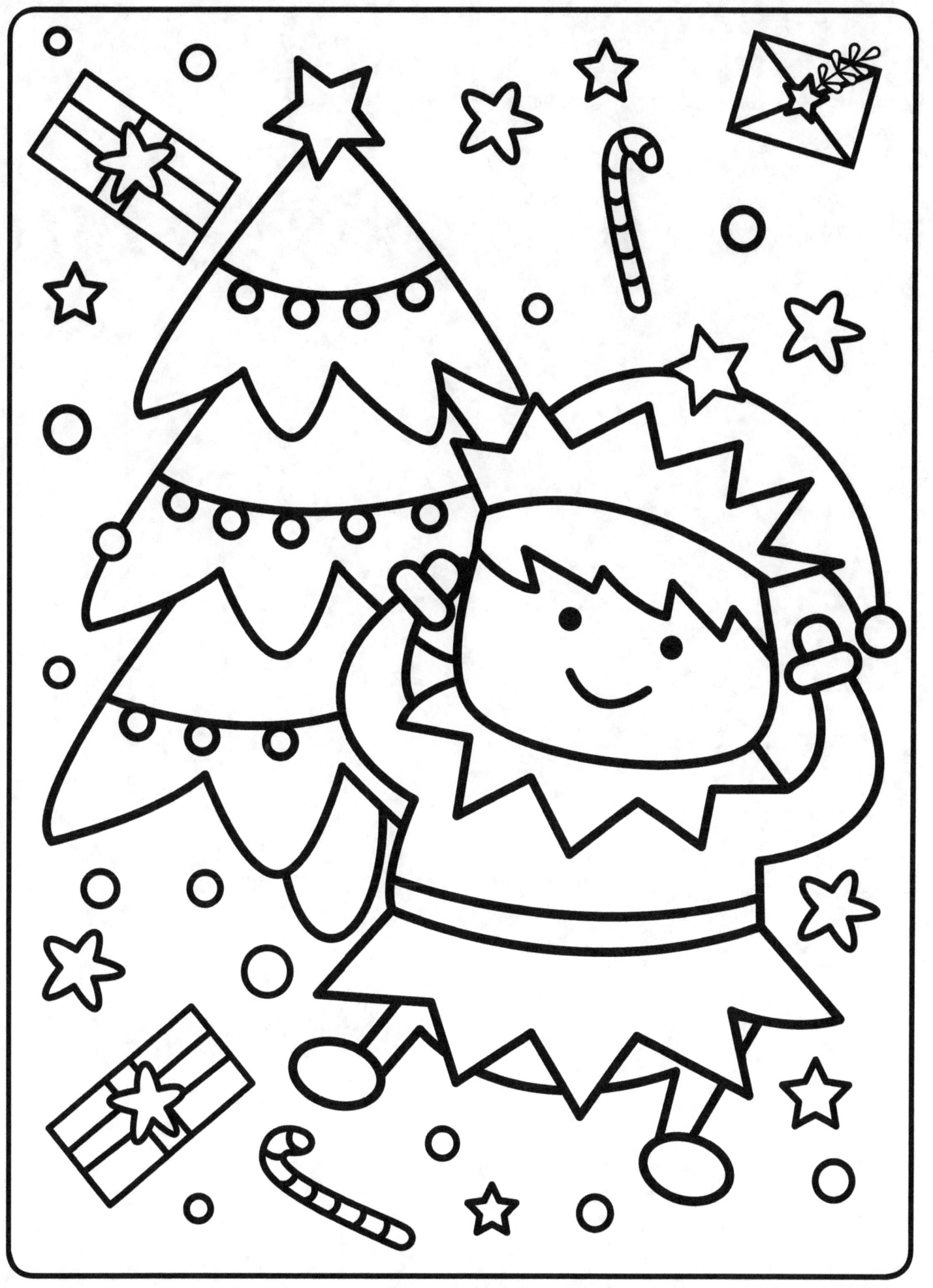

COLOR CHARTS TEST

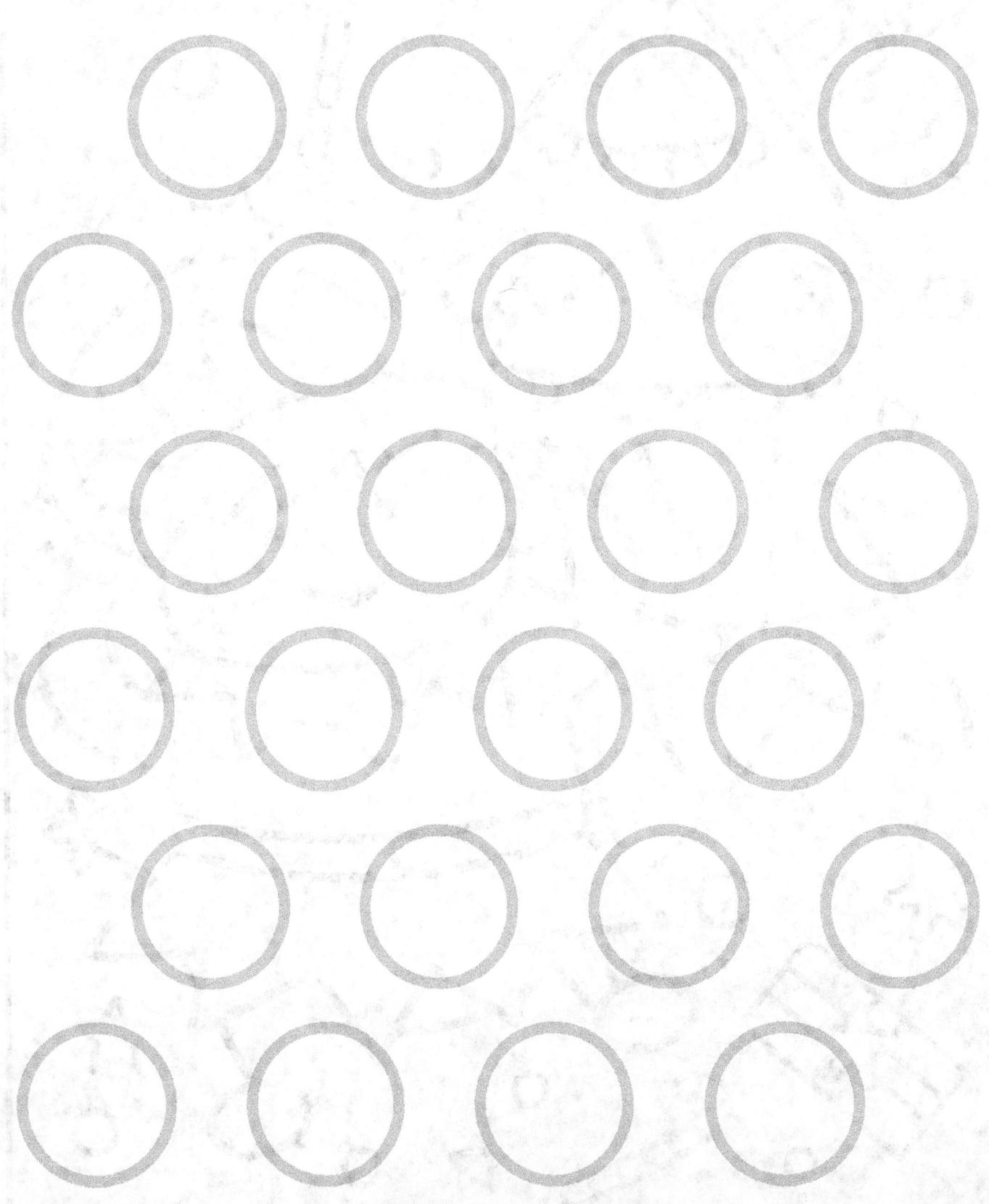

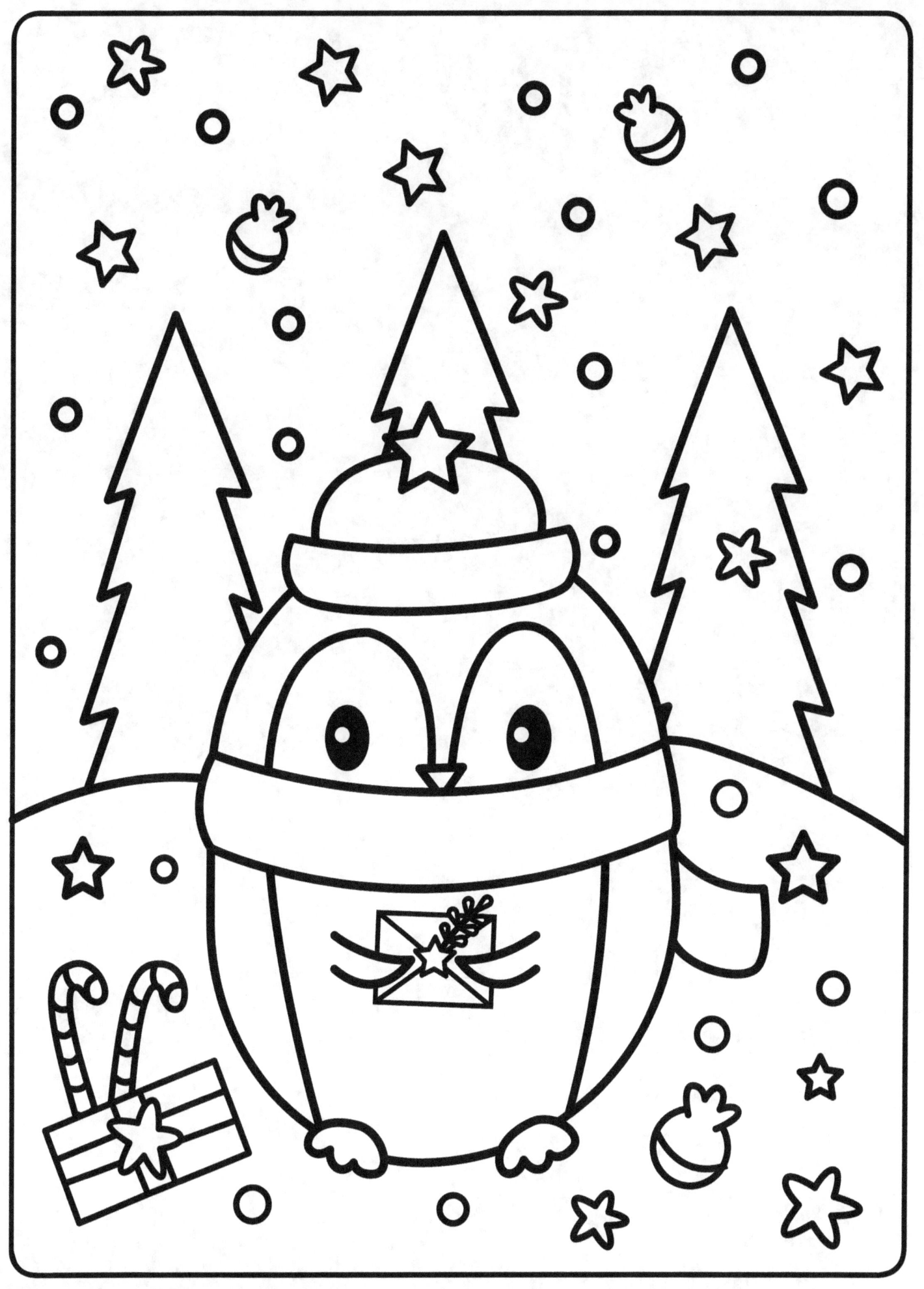

COLOR CHARTS TEST

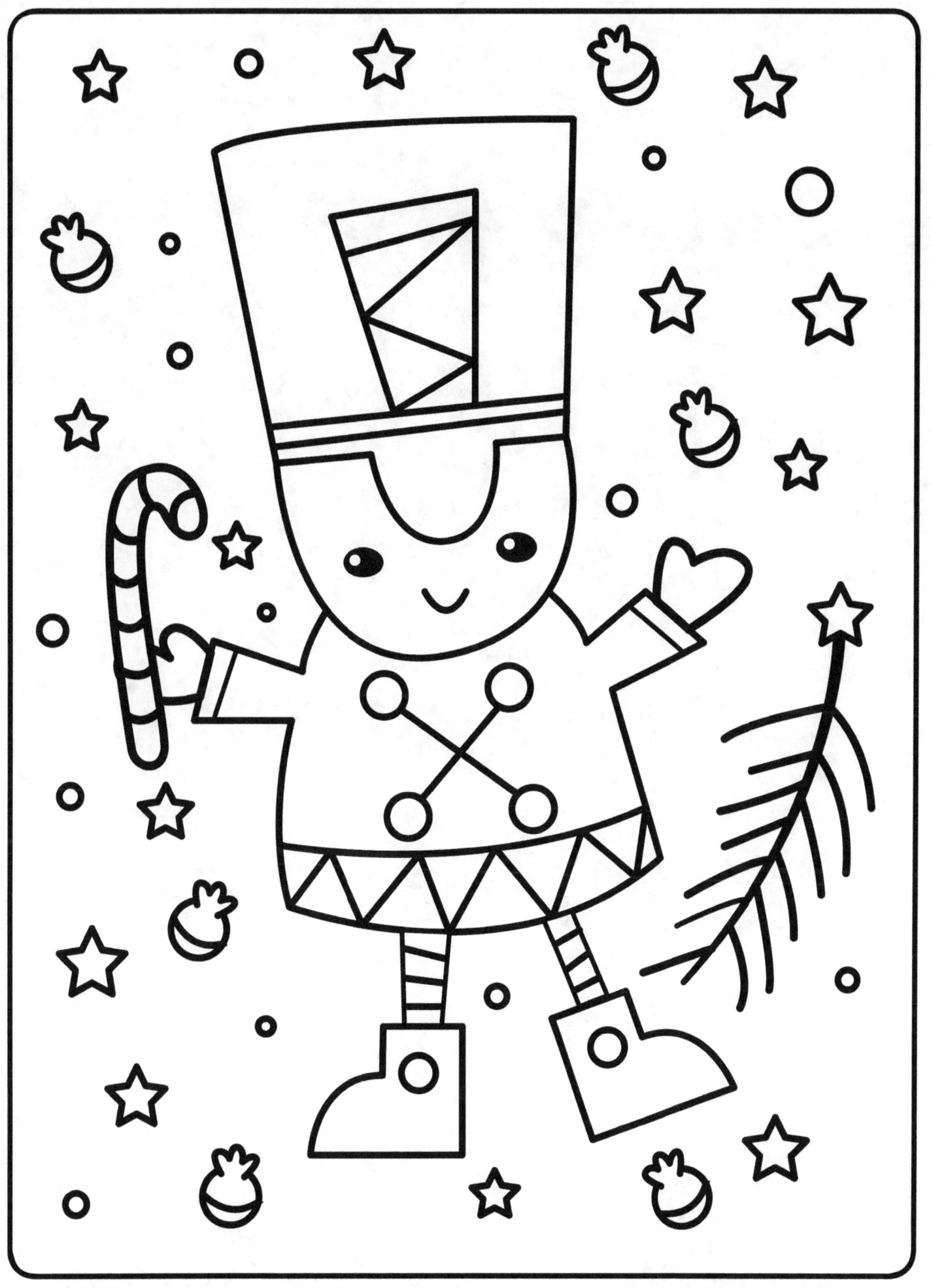

COLOR CHARTS TEST

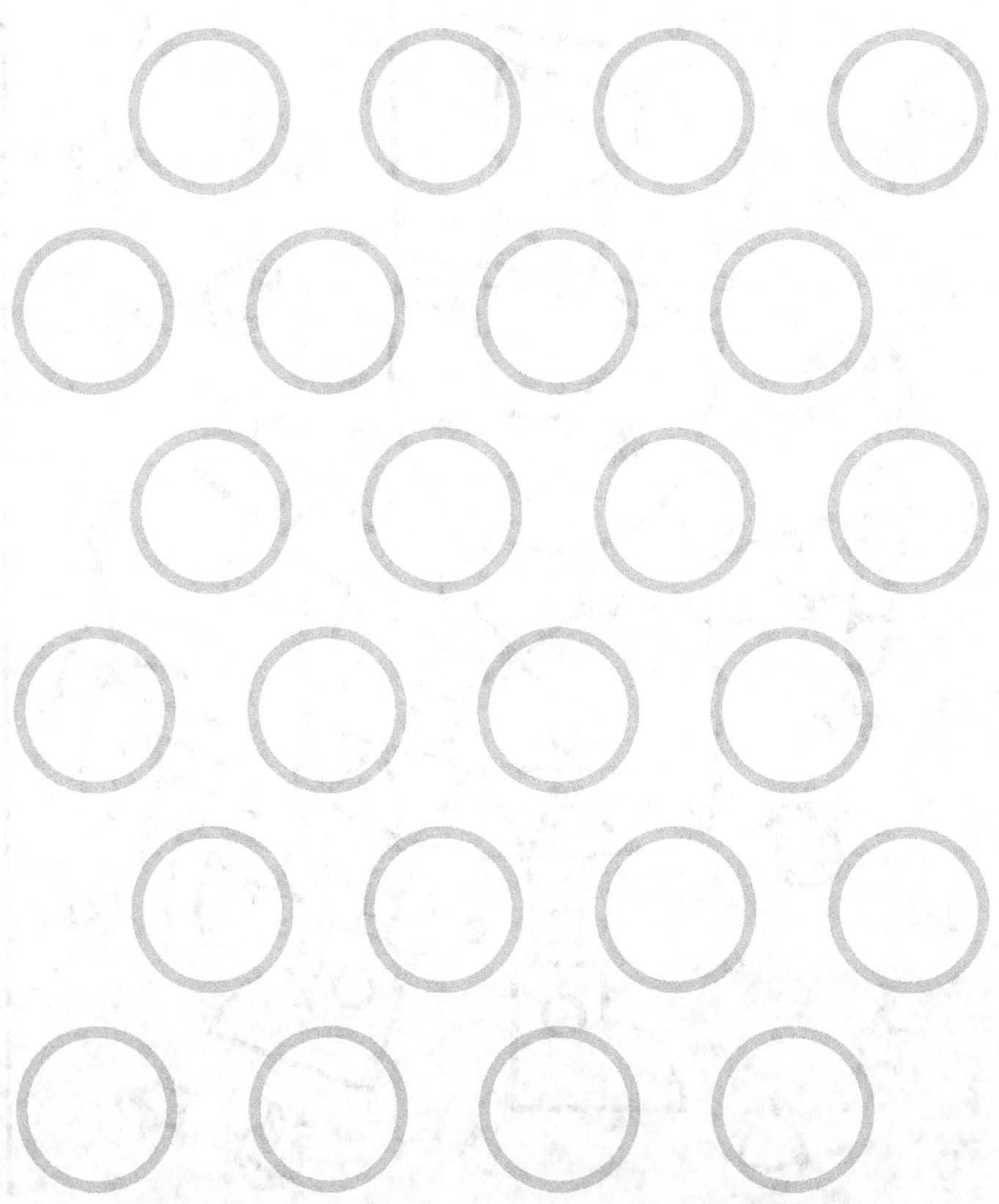

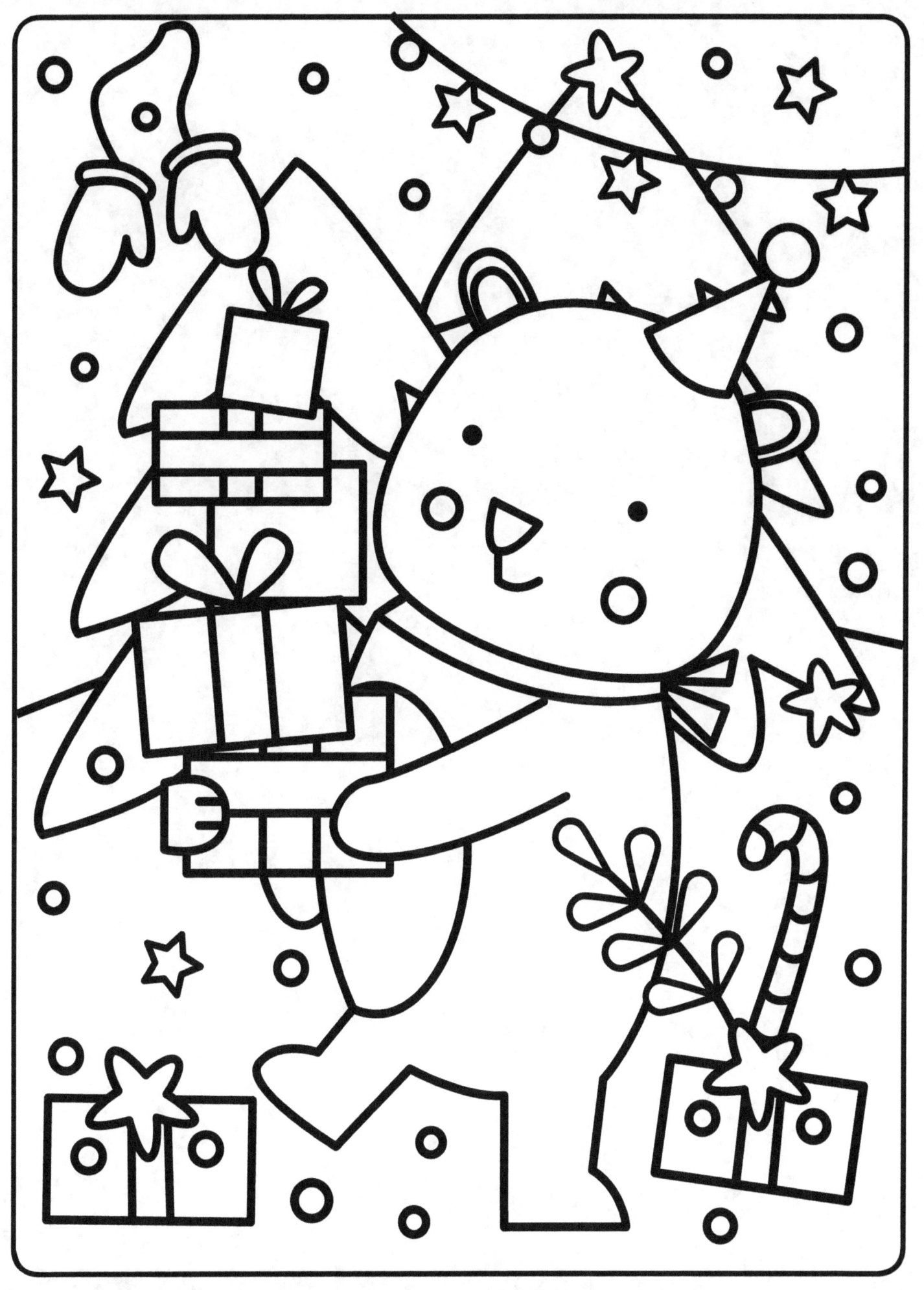

COLOR CHARTS TEST

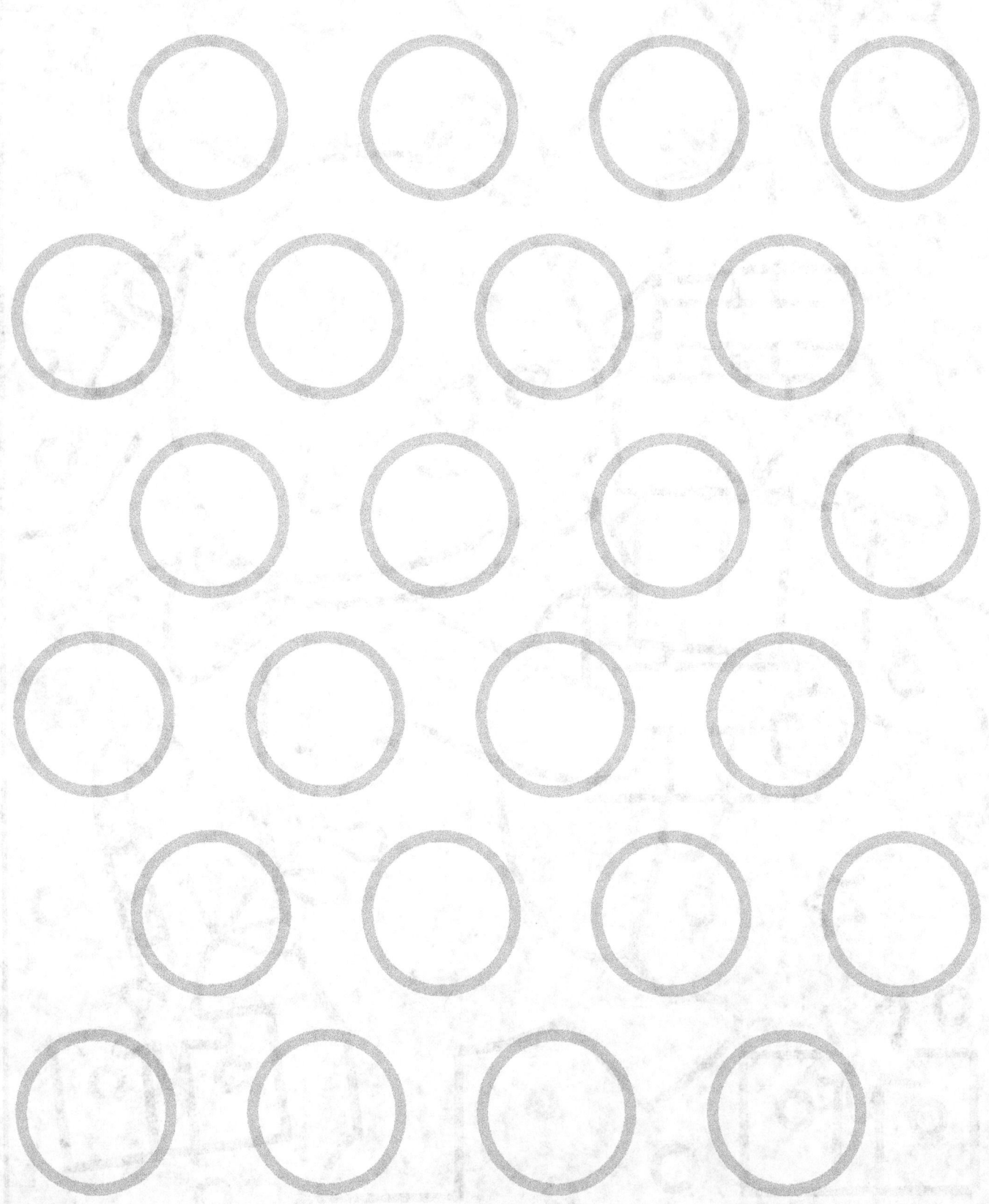

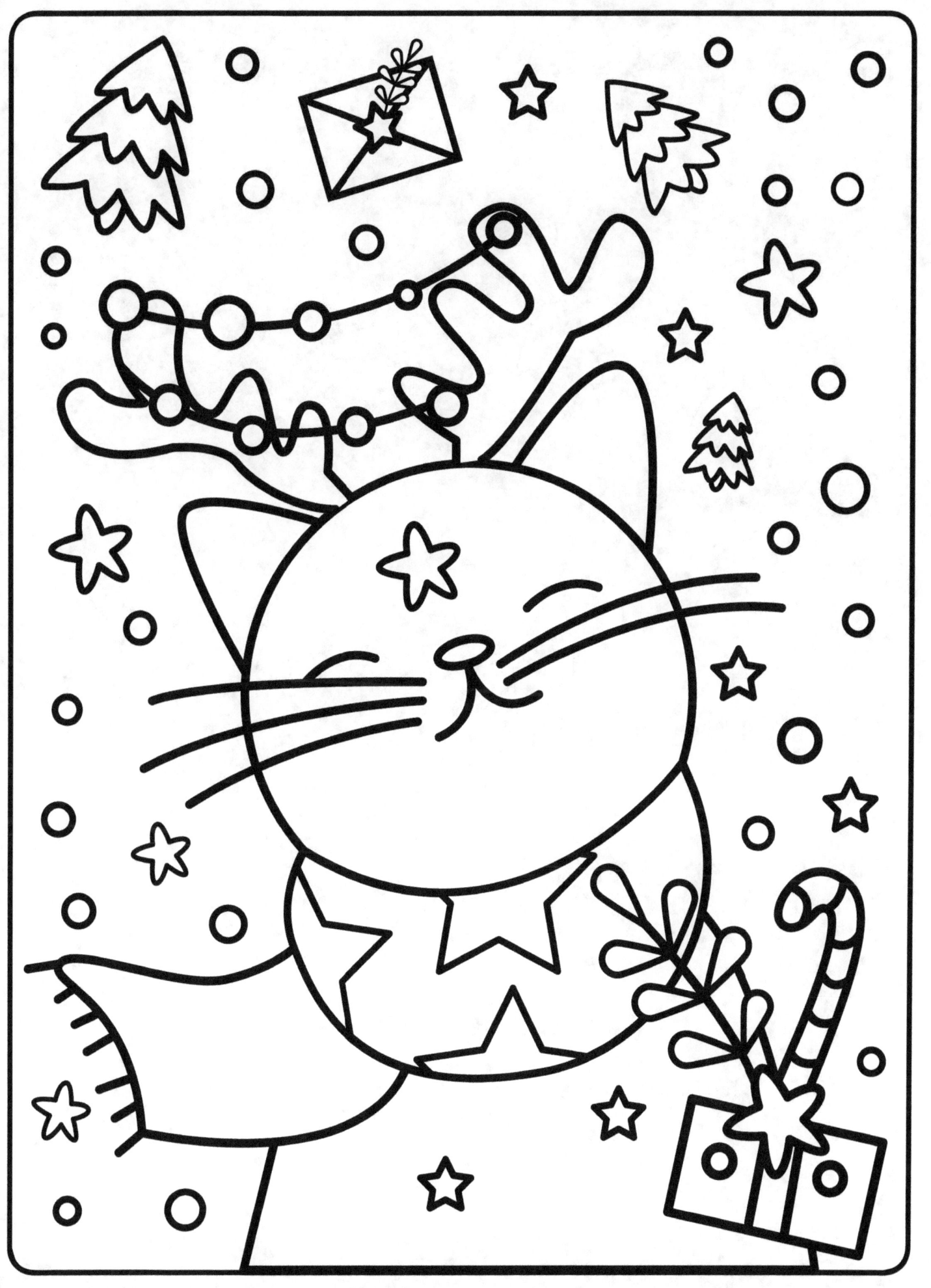

COLOR CHARTS TEST

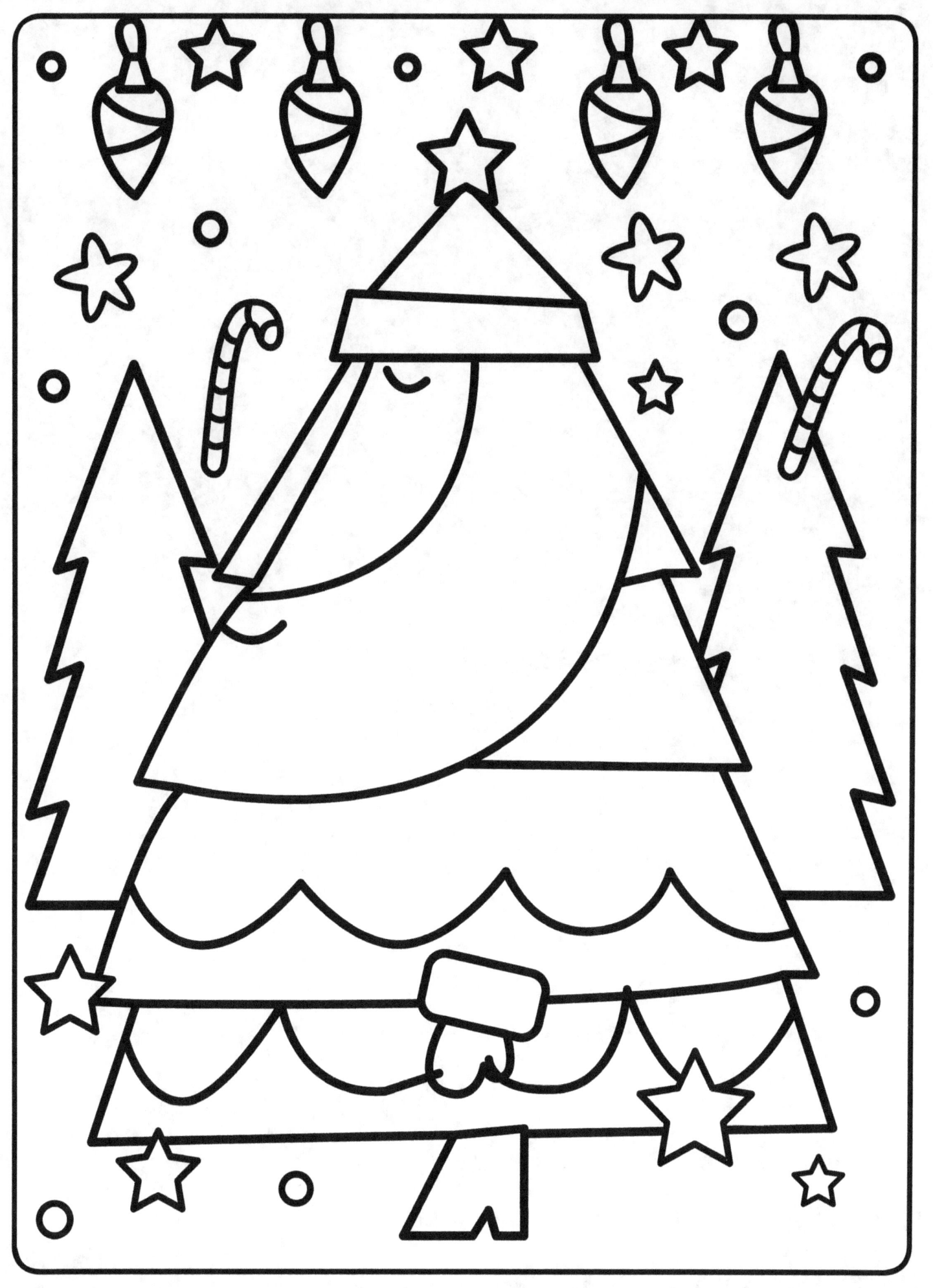

COLOR CHARTS TEST

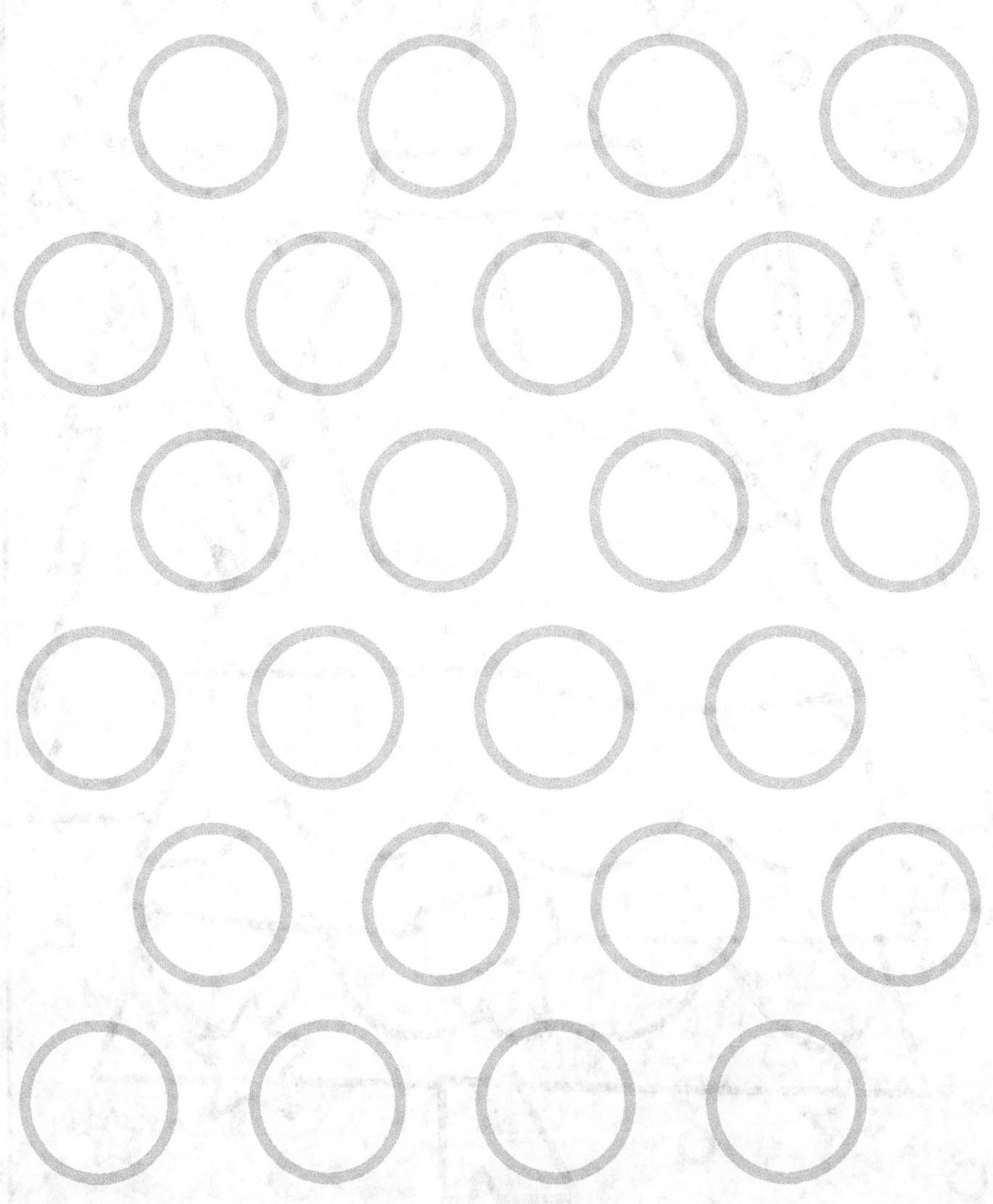

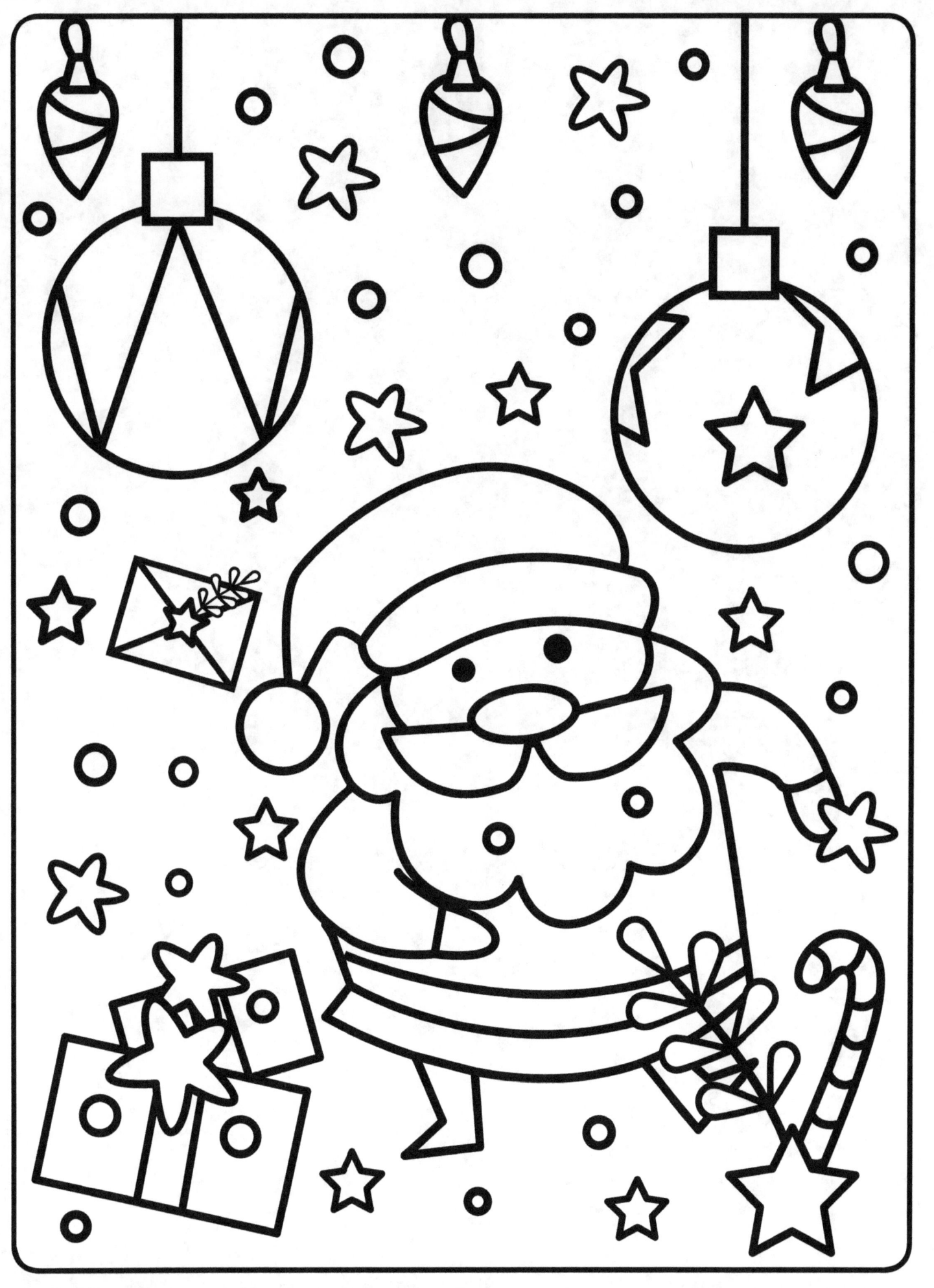

COLOR CHARTS TEST

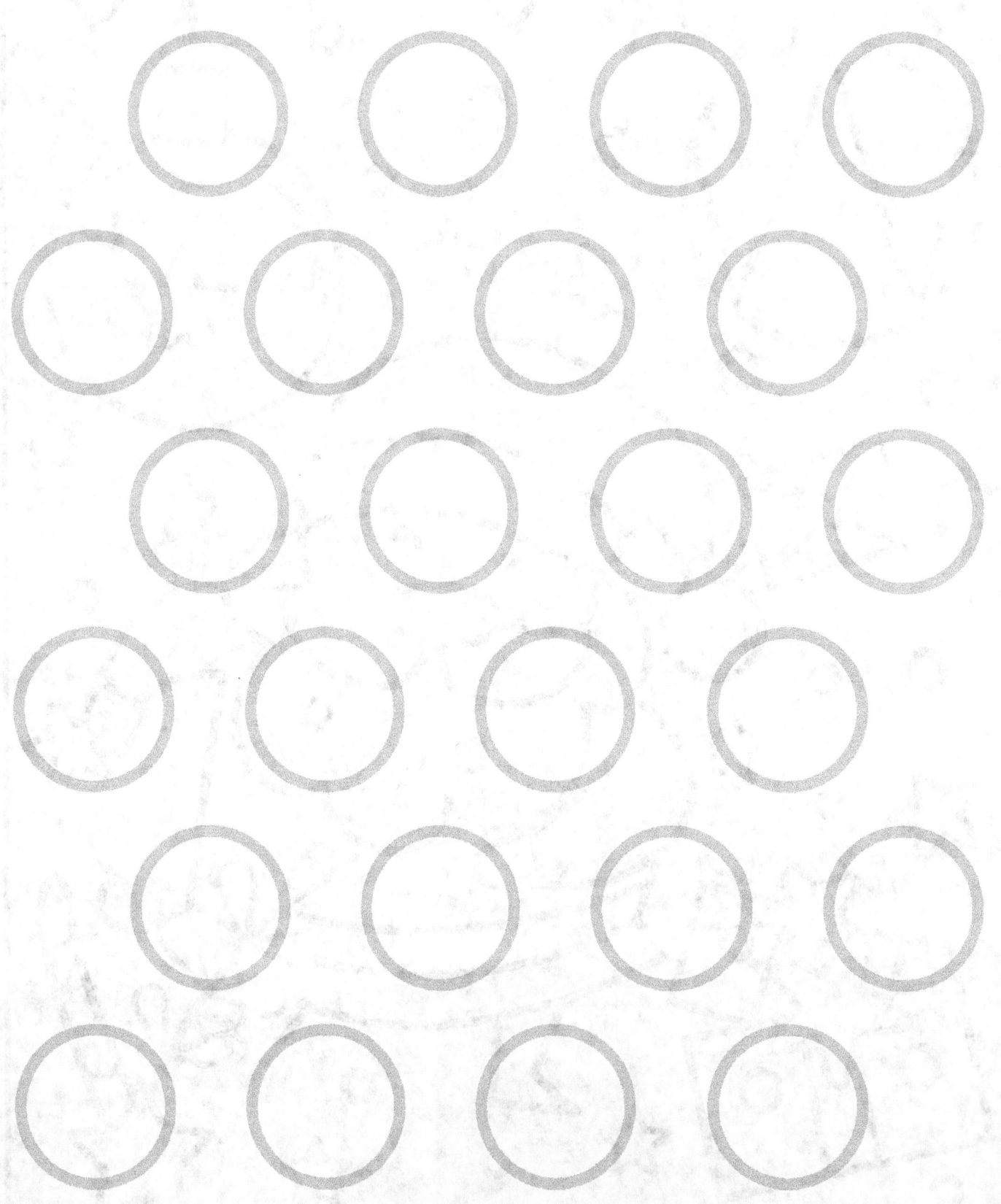

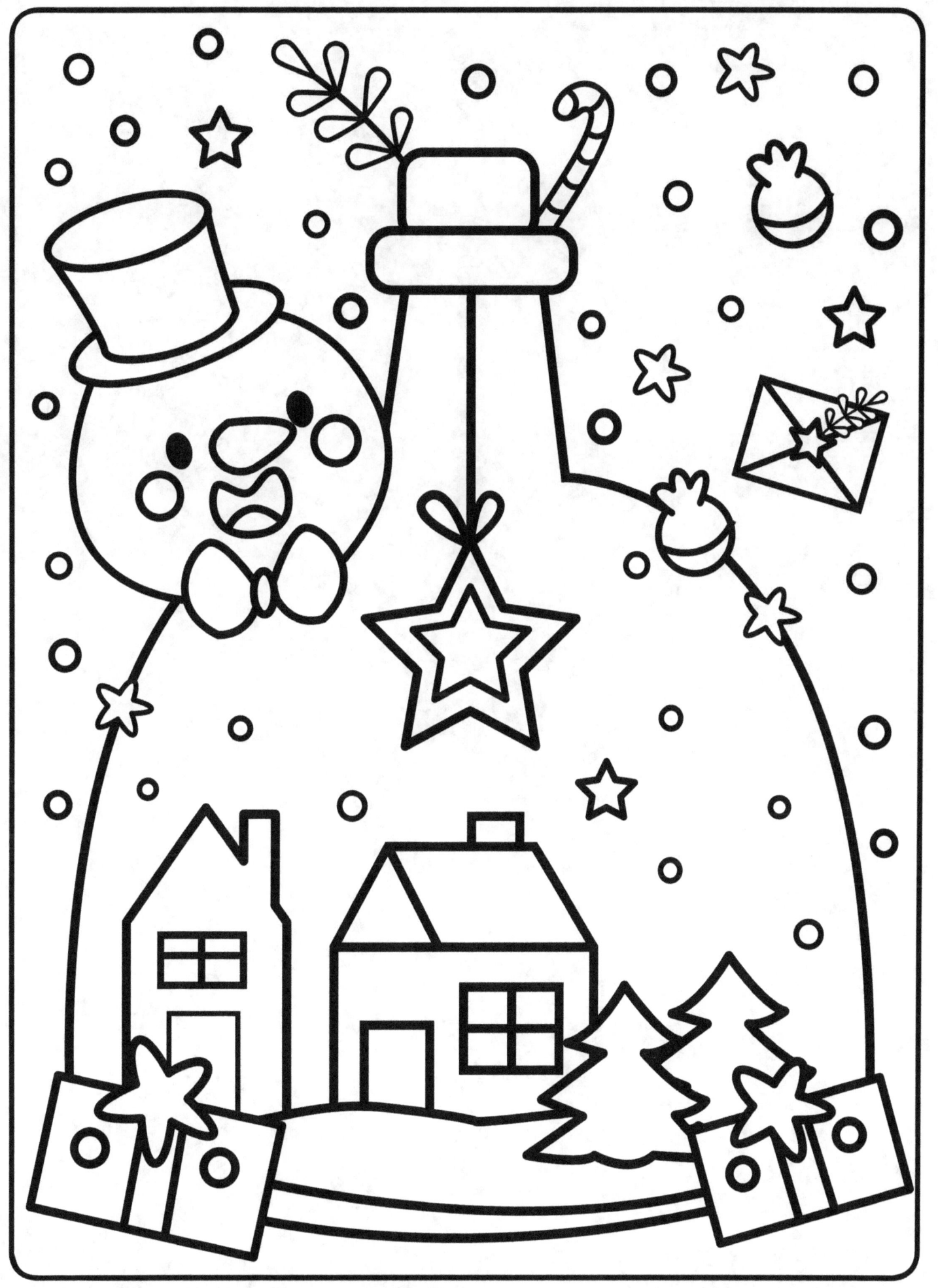

COLOR CHARTS TEST

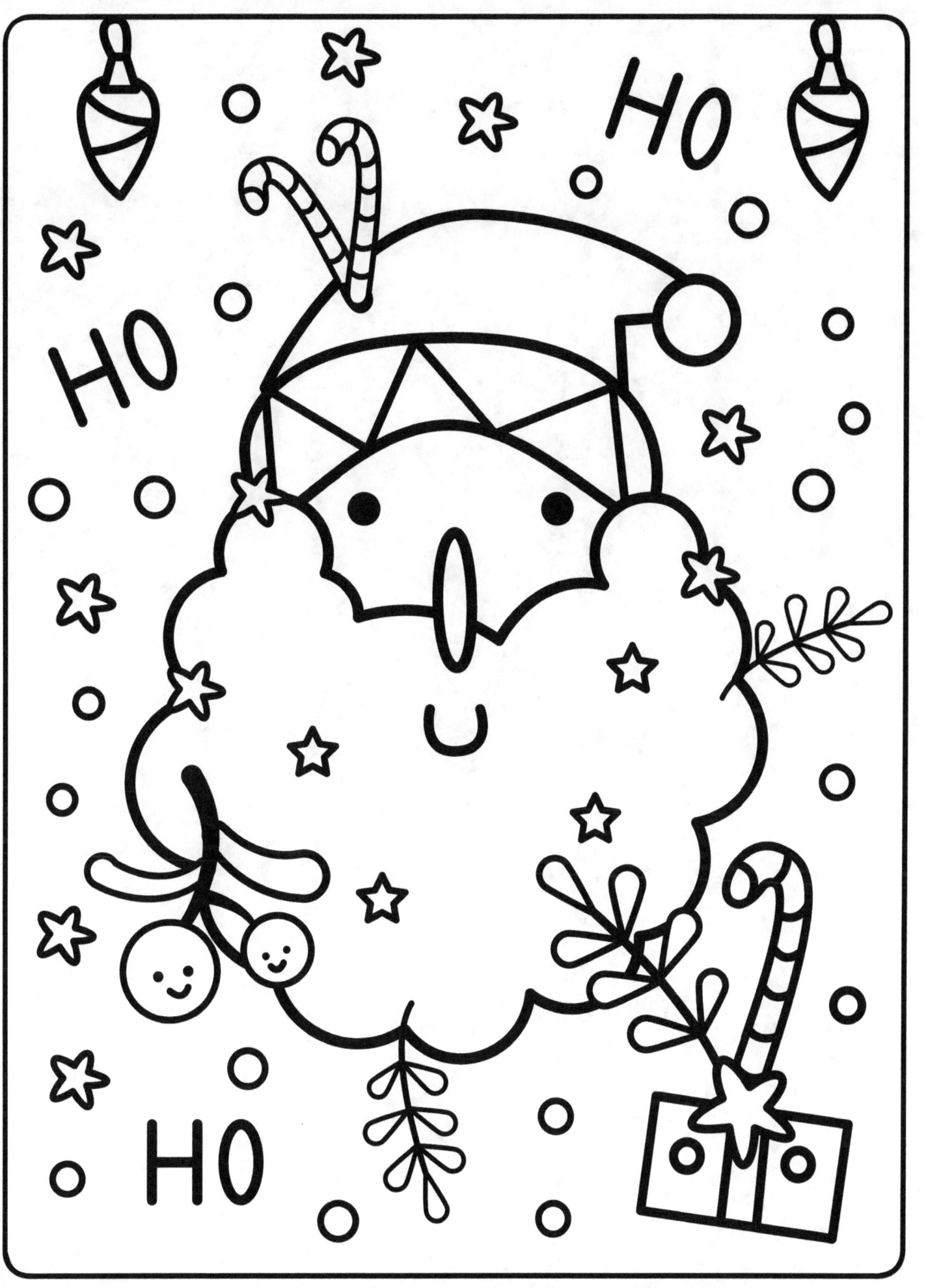

COLOR CHARTS TEST

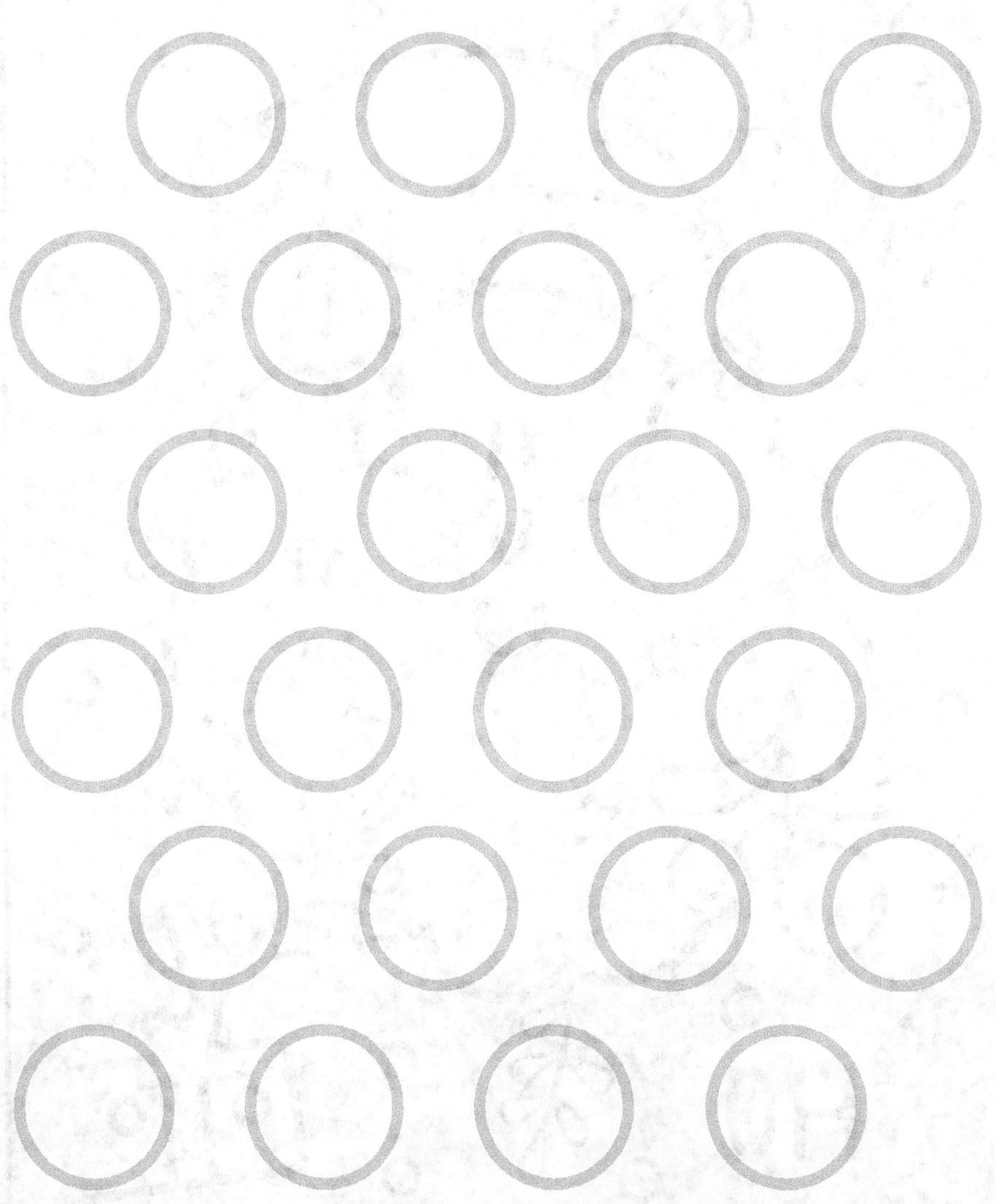

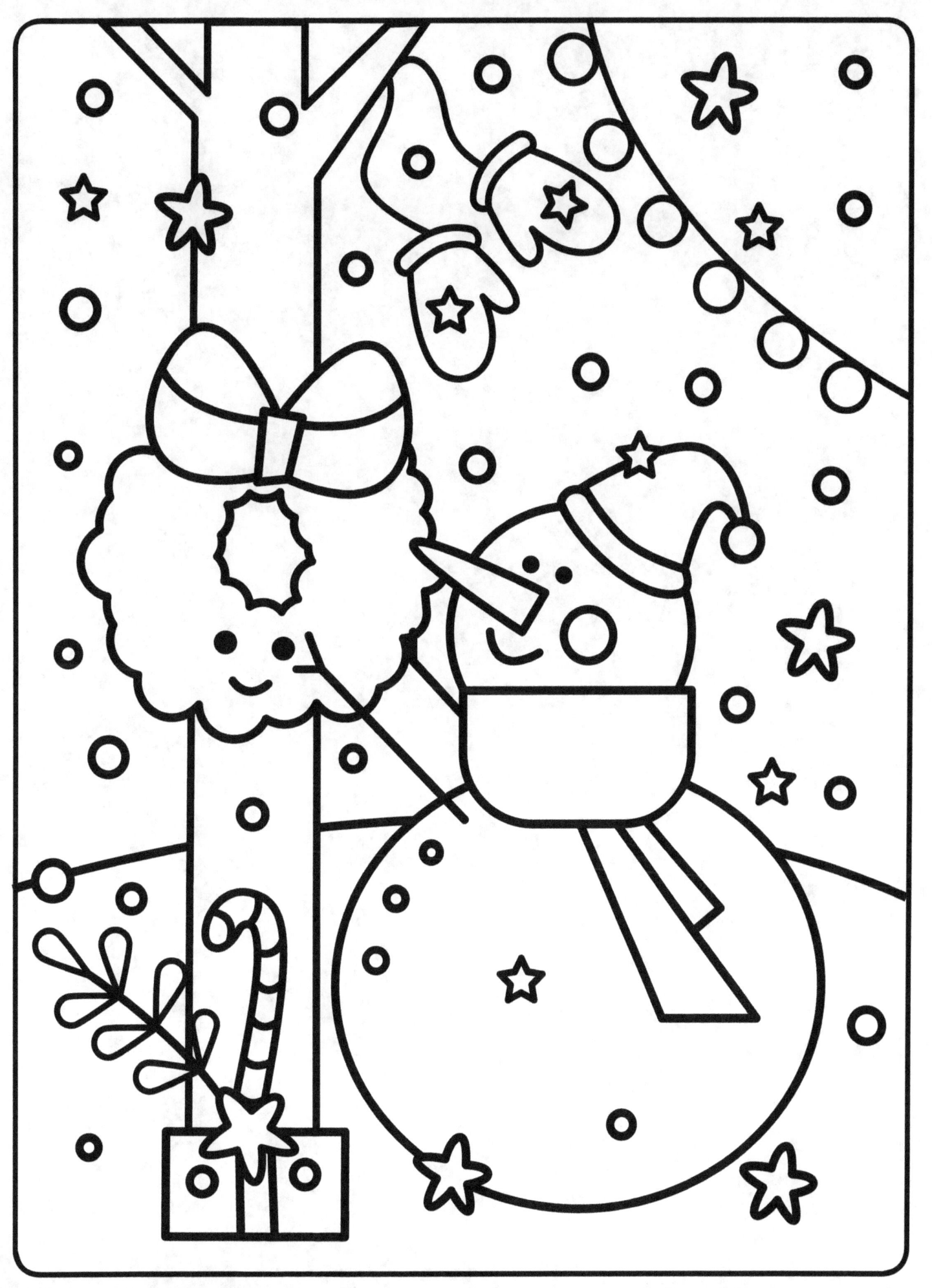

COLOR CHARTS TEST

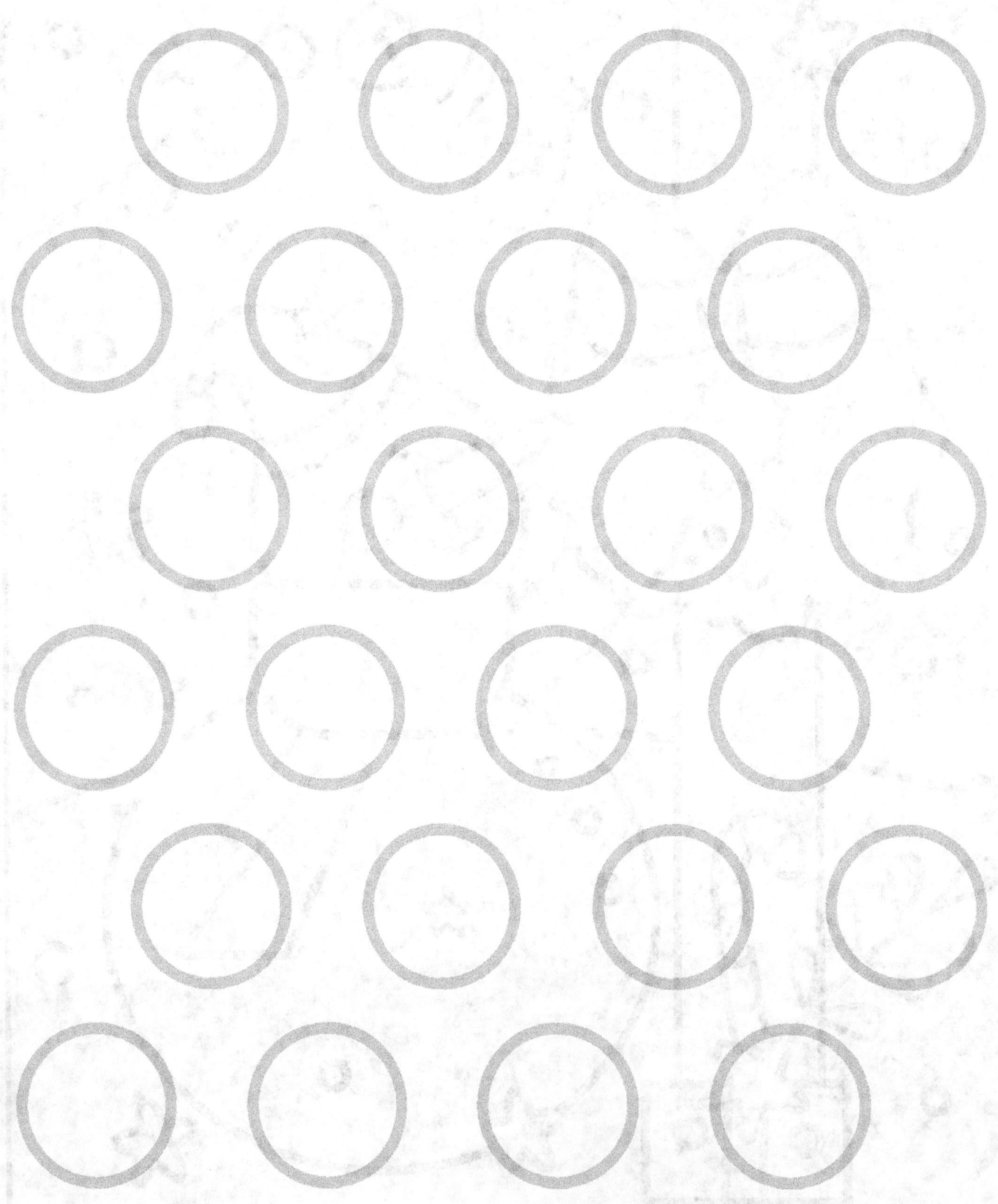

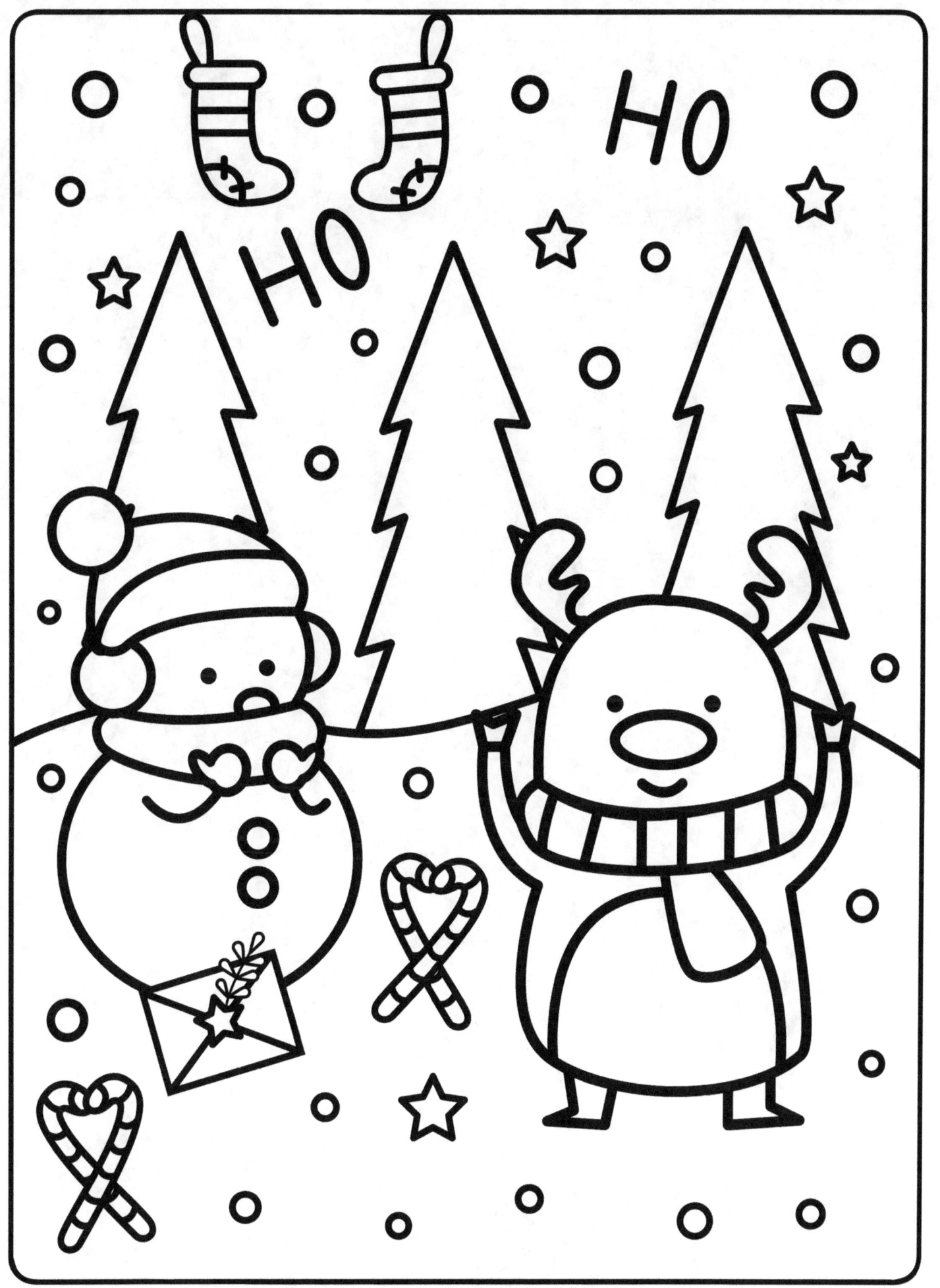

COLOR CHARTS TEST

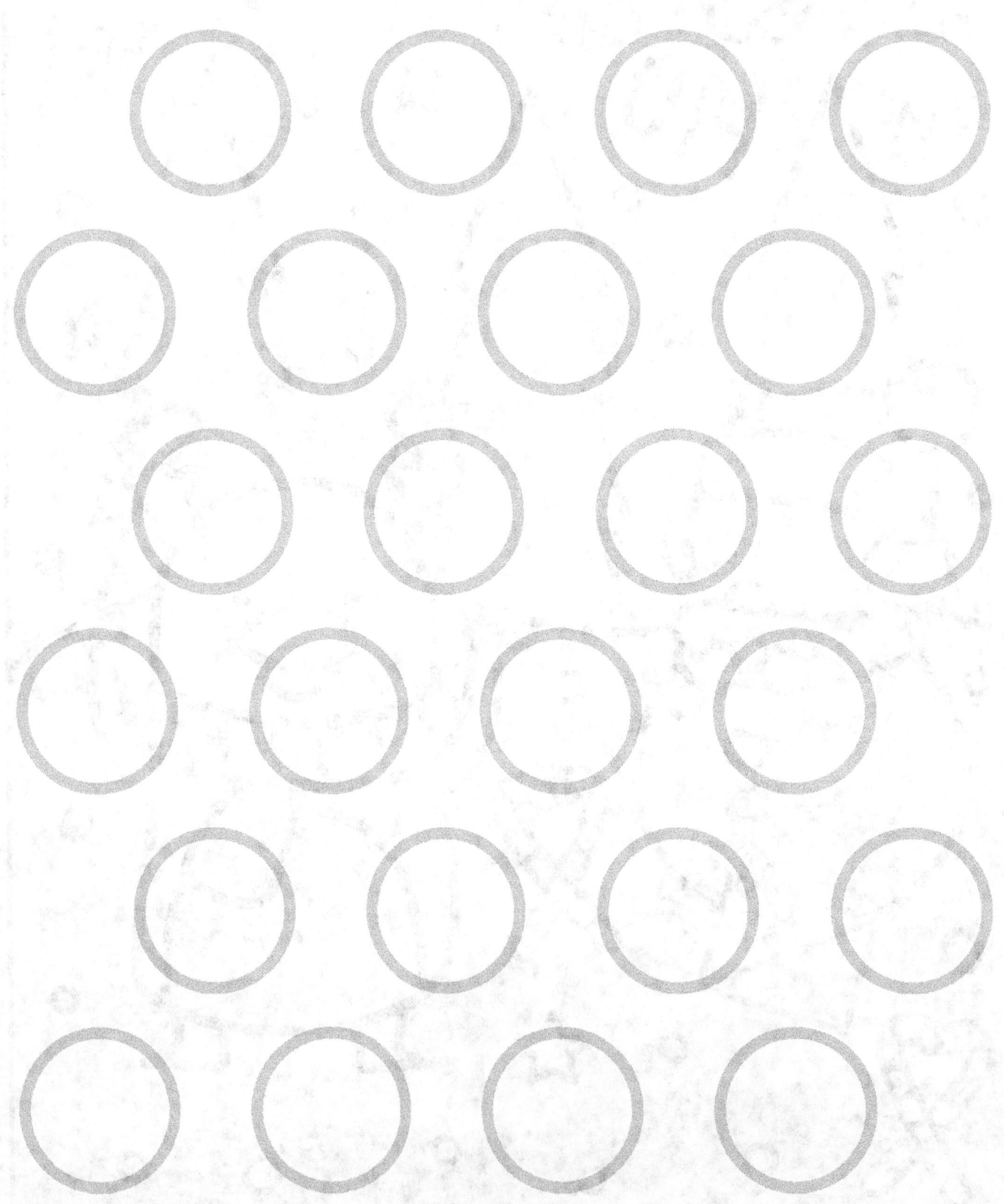

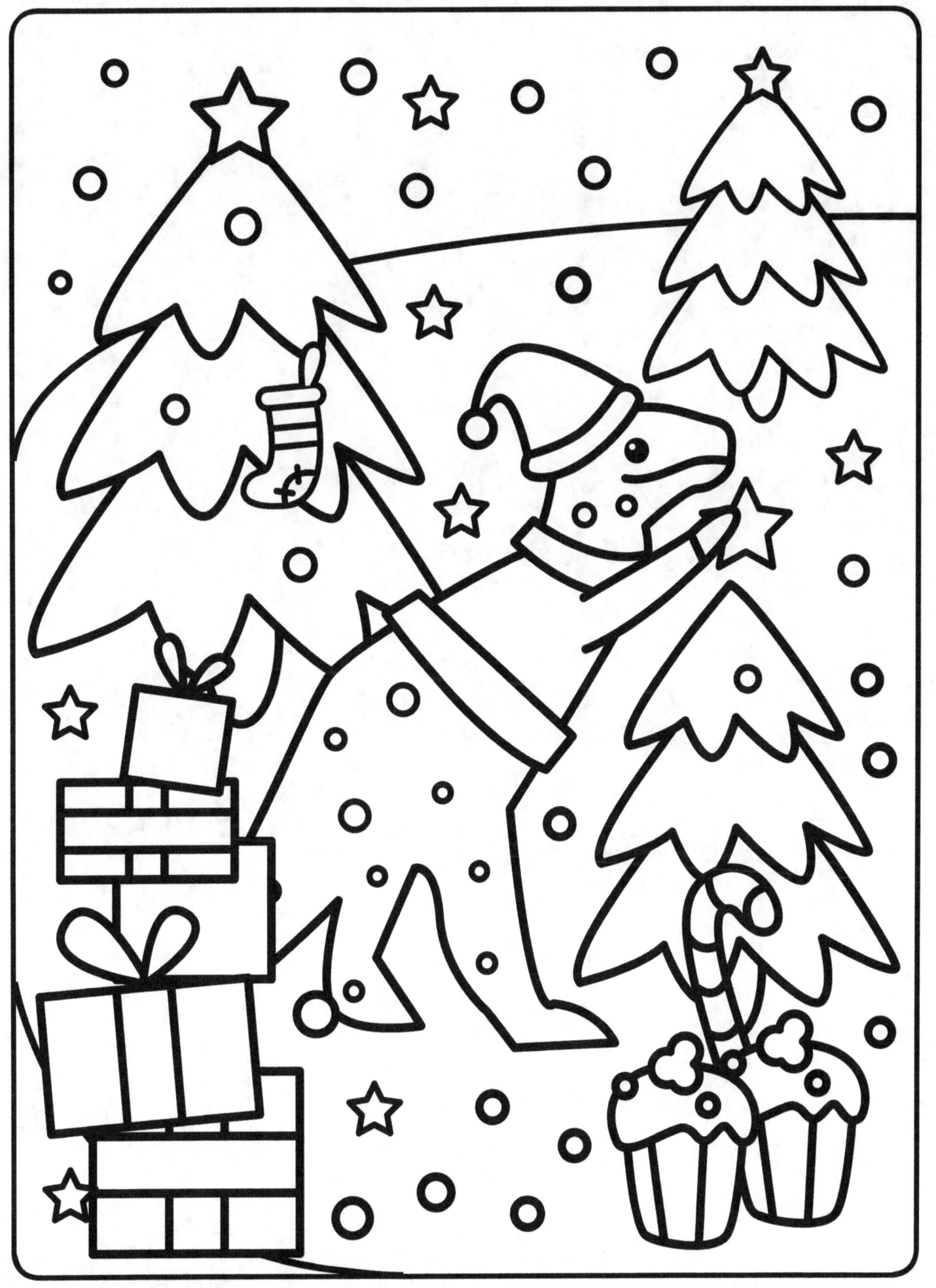

COLOR CHARTS TEST

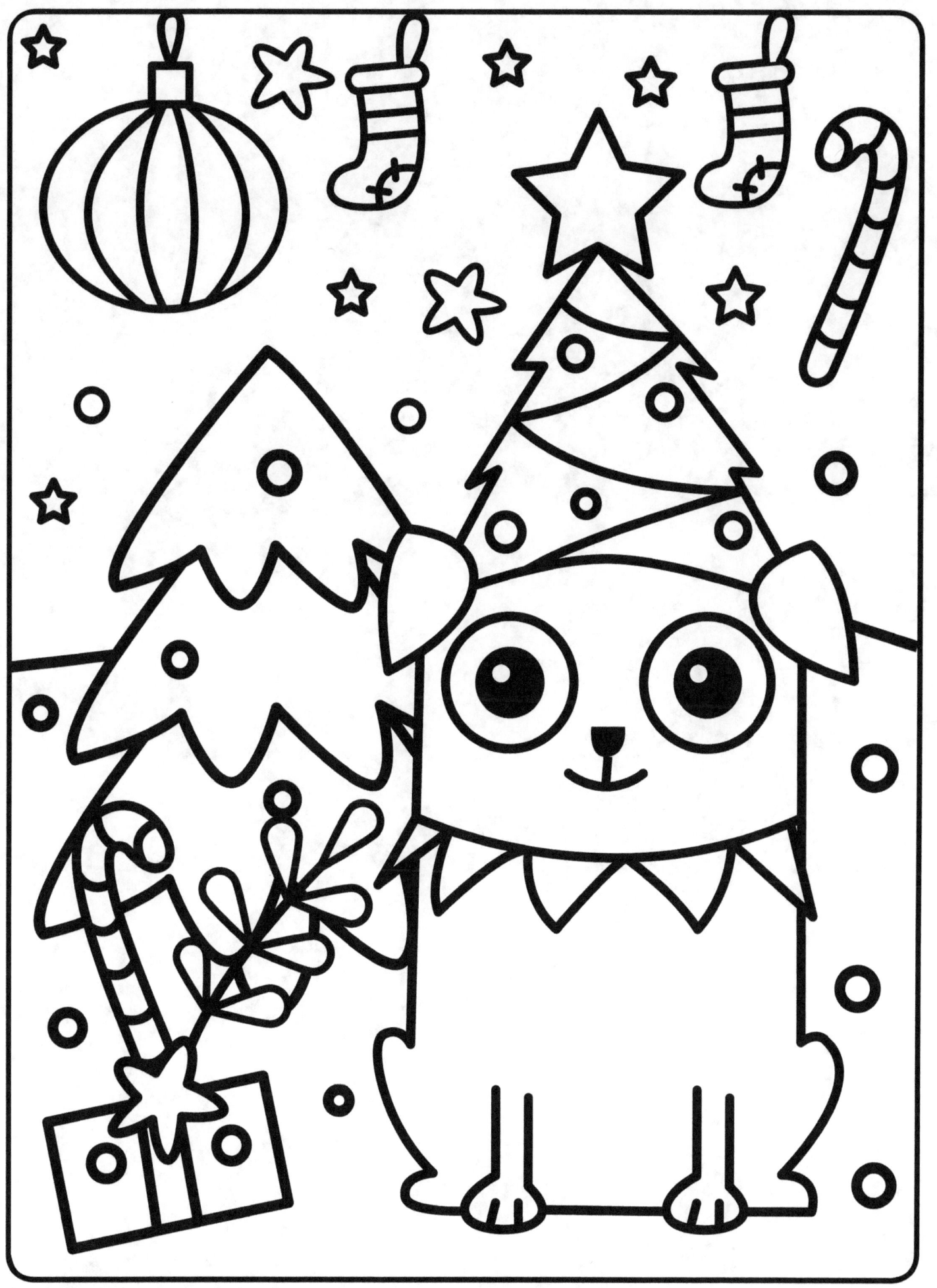

COLOR CHARTS TEST

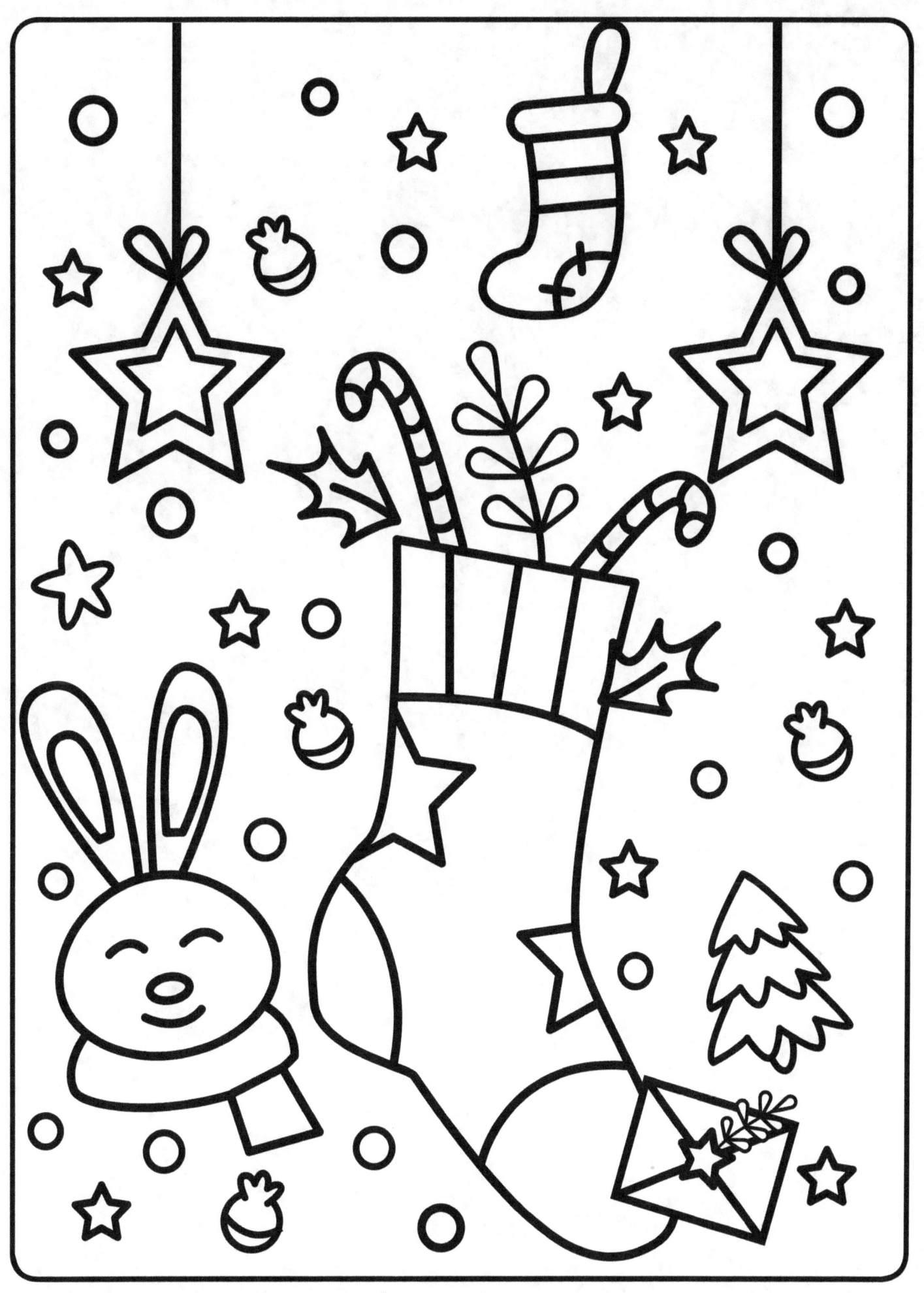

COLOR CHARTS TEST

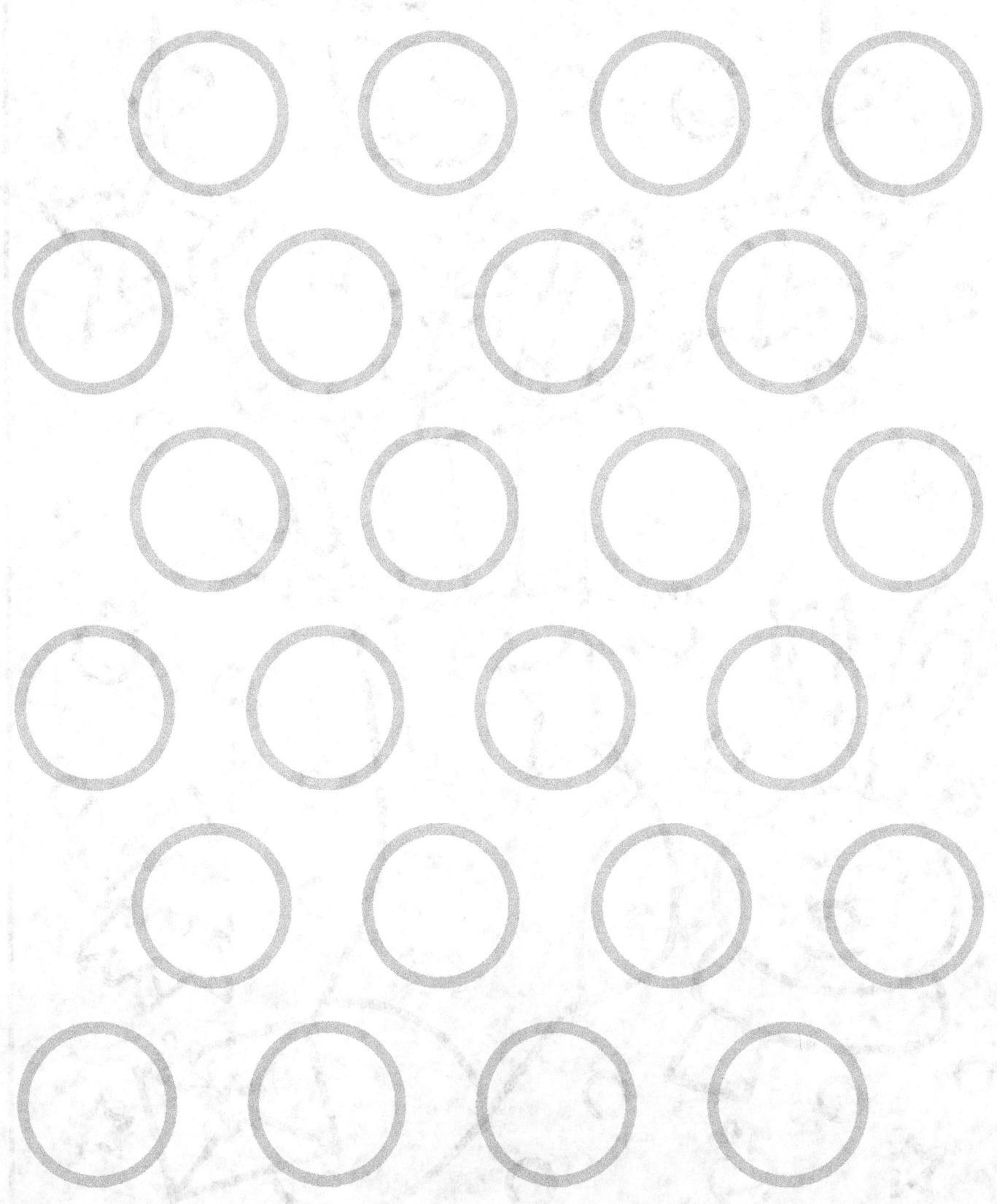

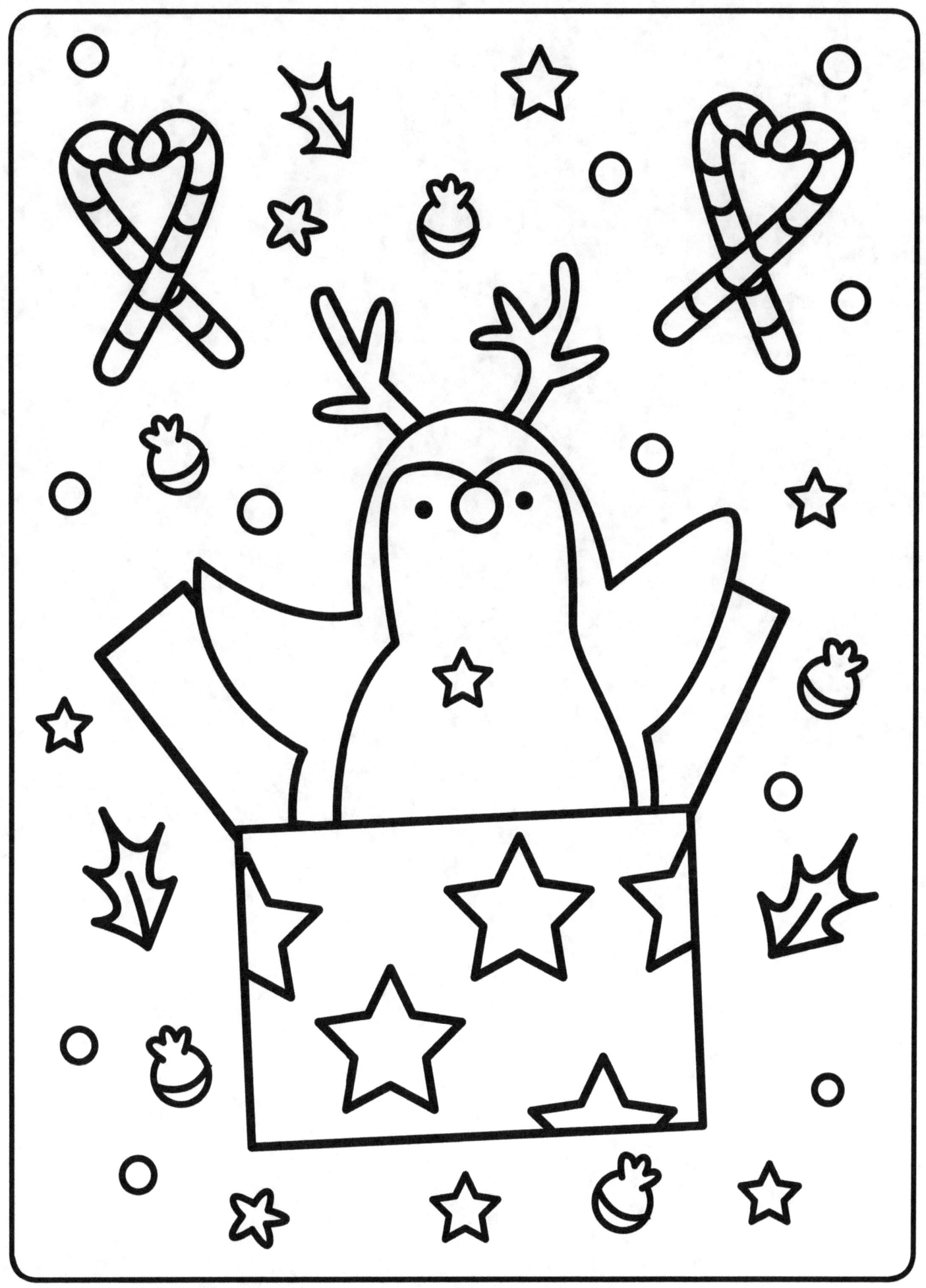

COLOR CHARTS TEST

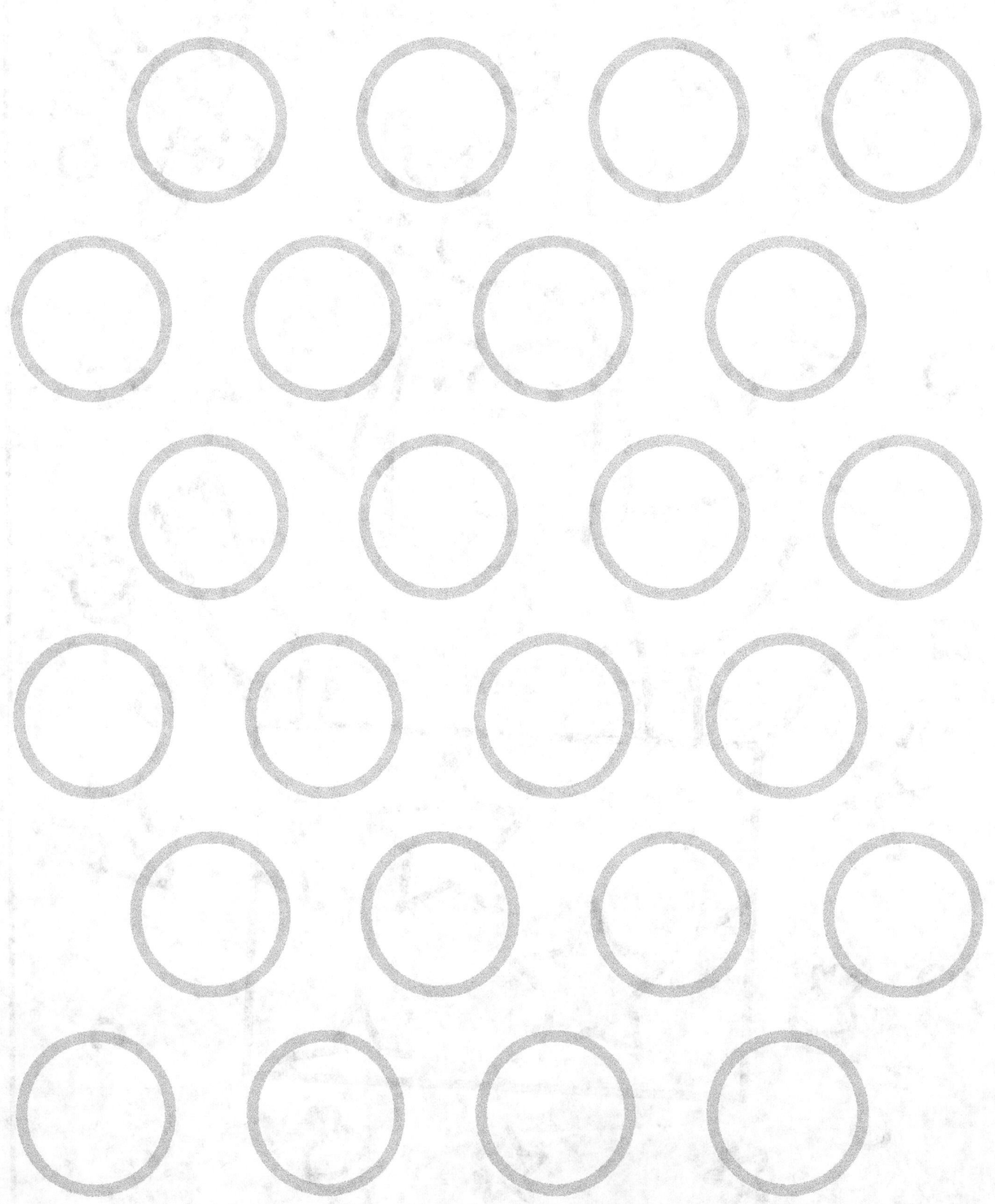

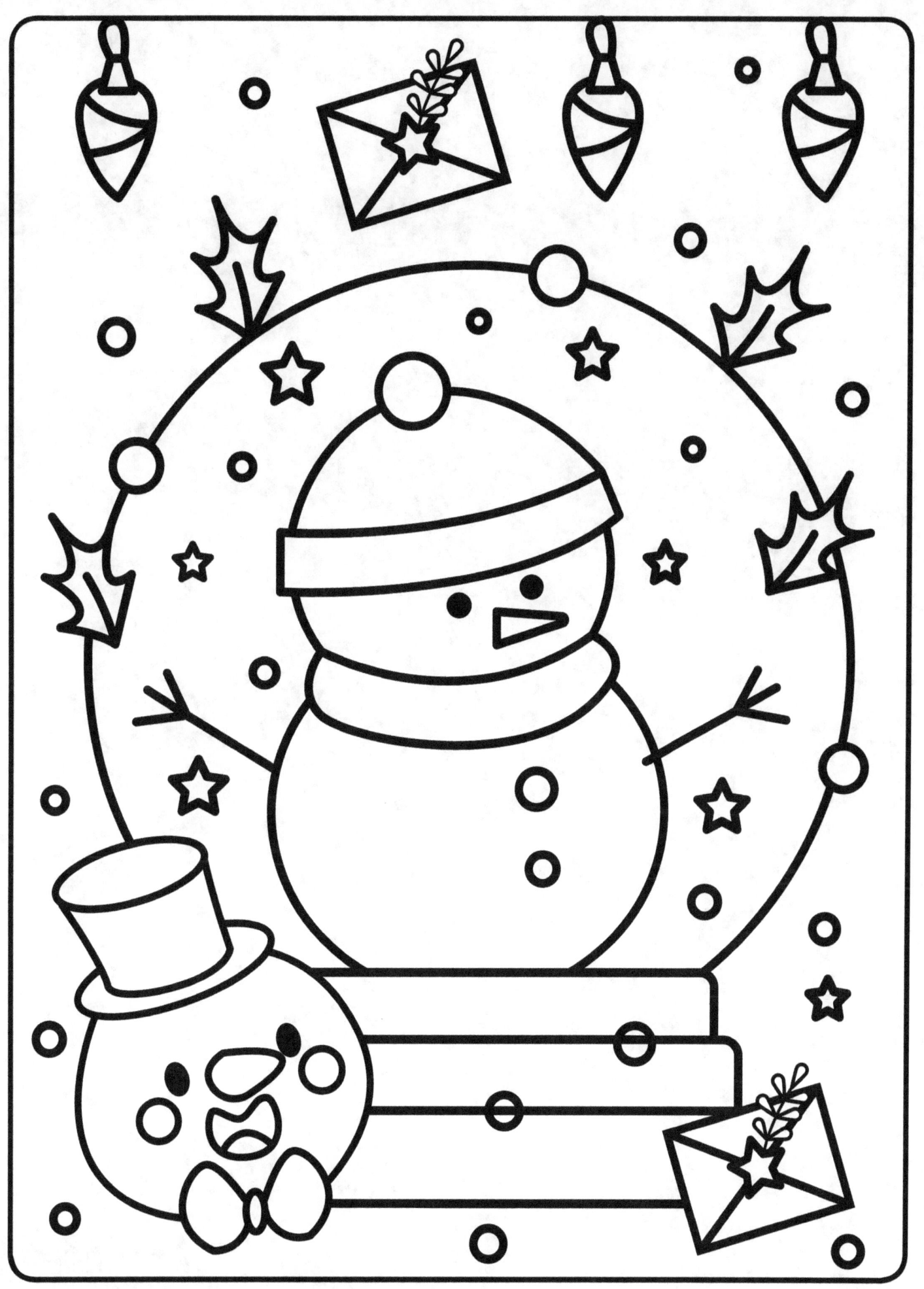

COLOR CHARTS TEST

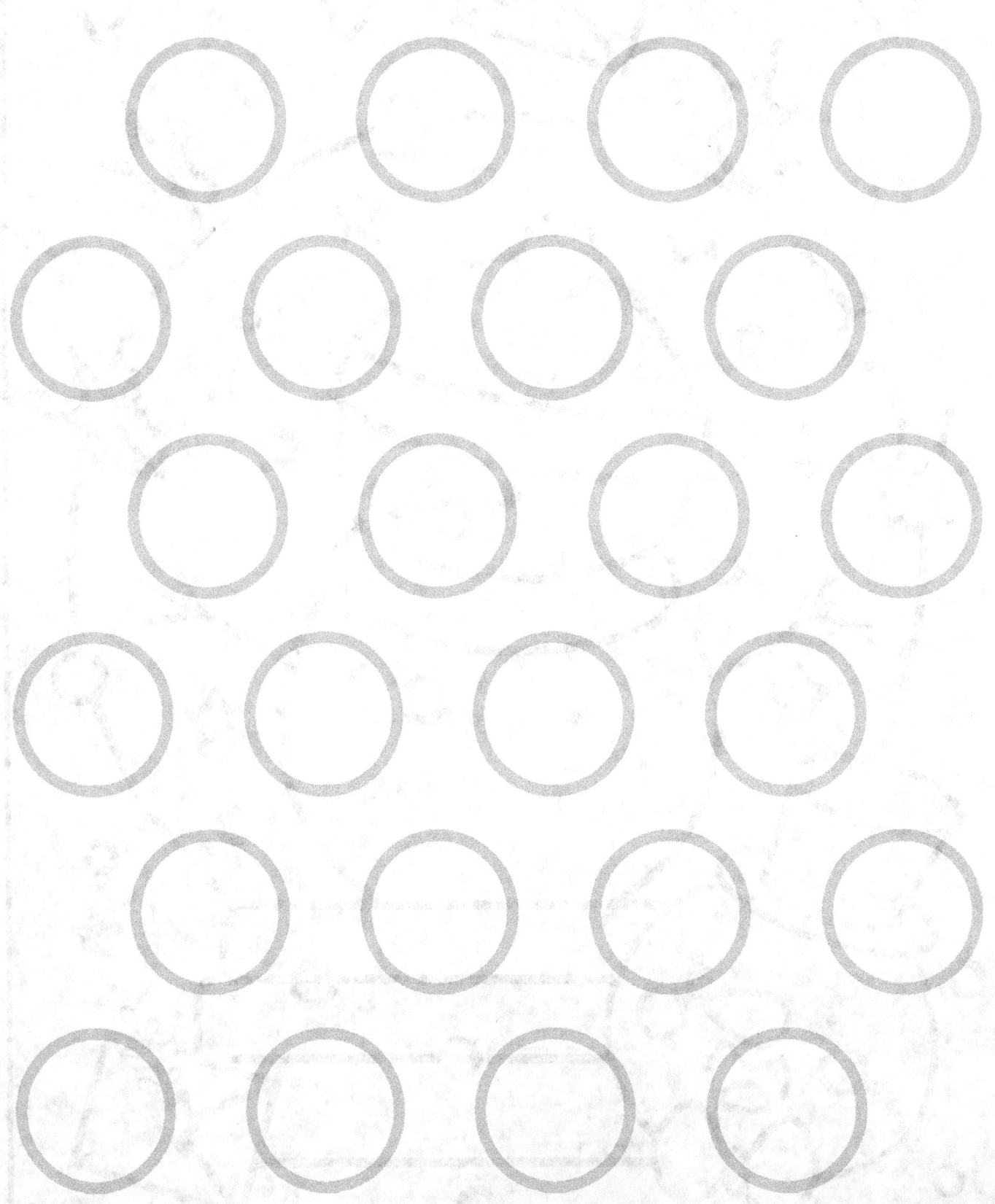

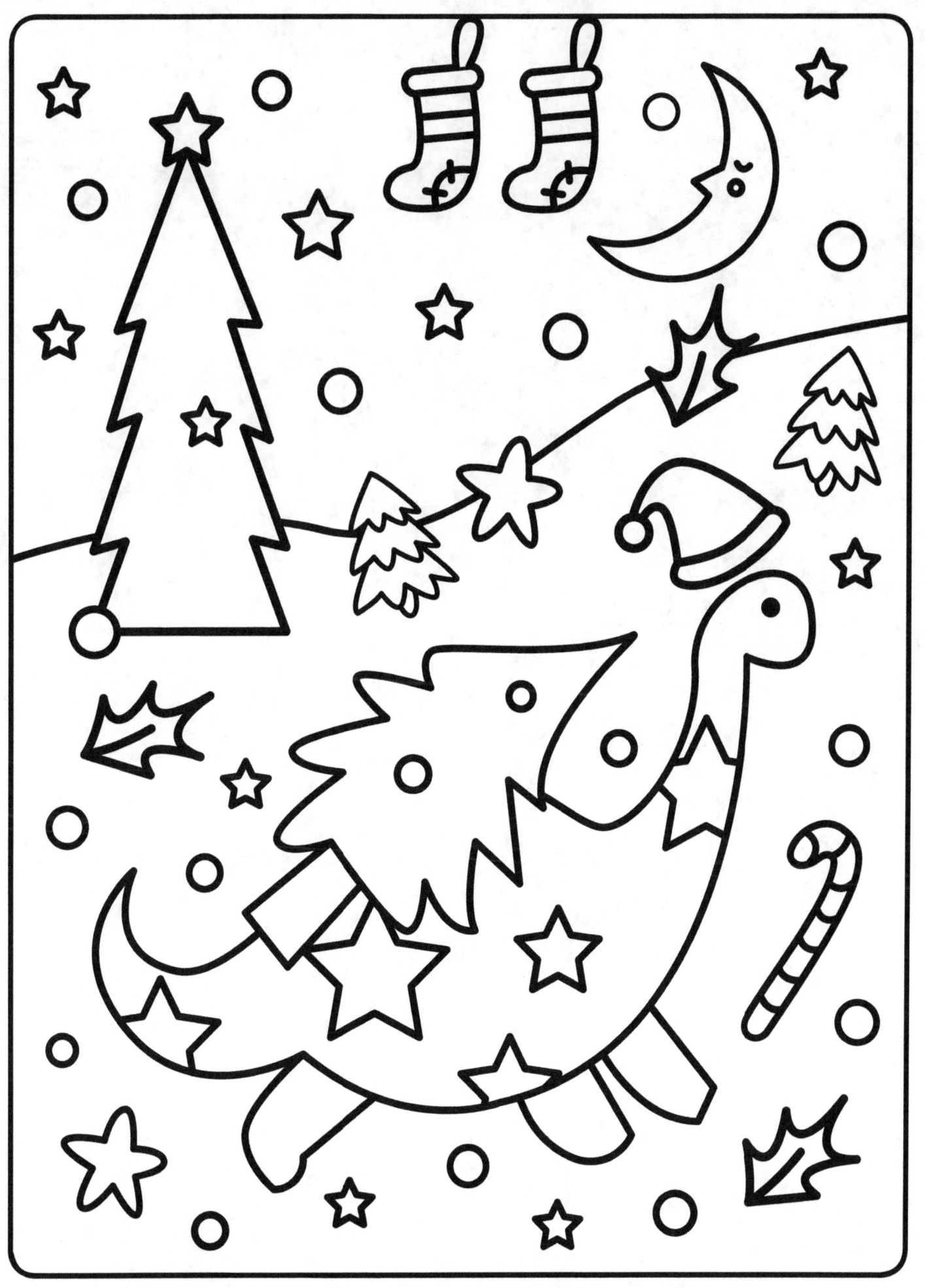

COLOR CHARTS TEST

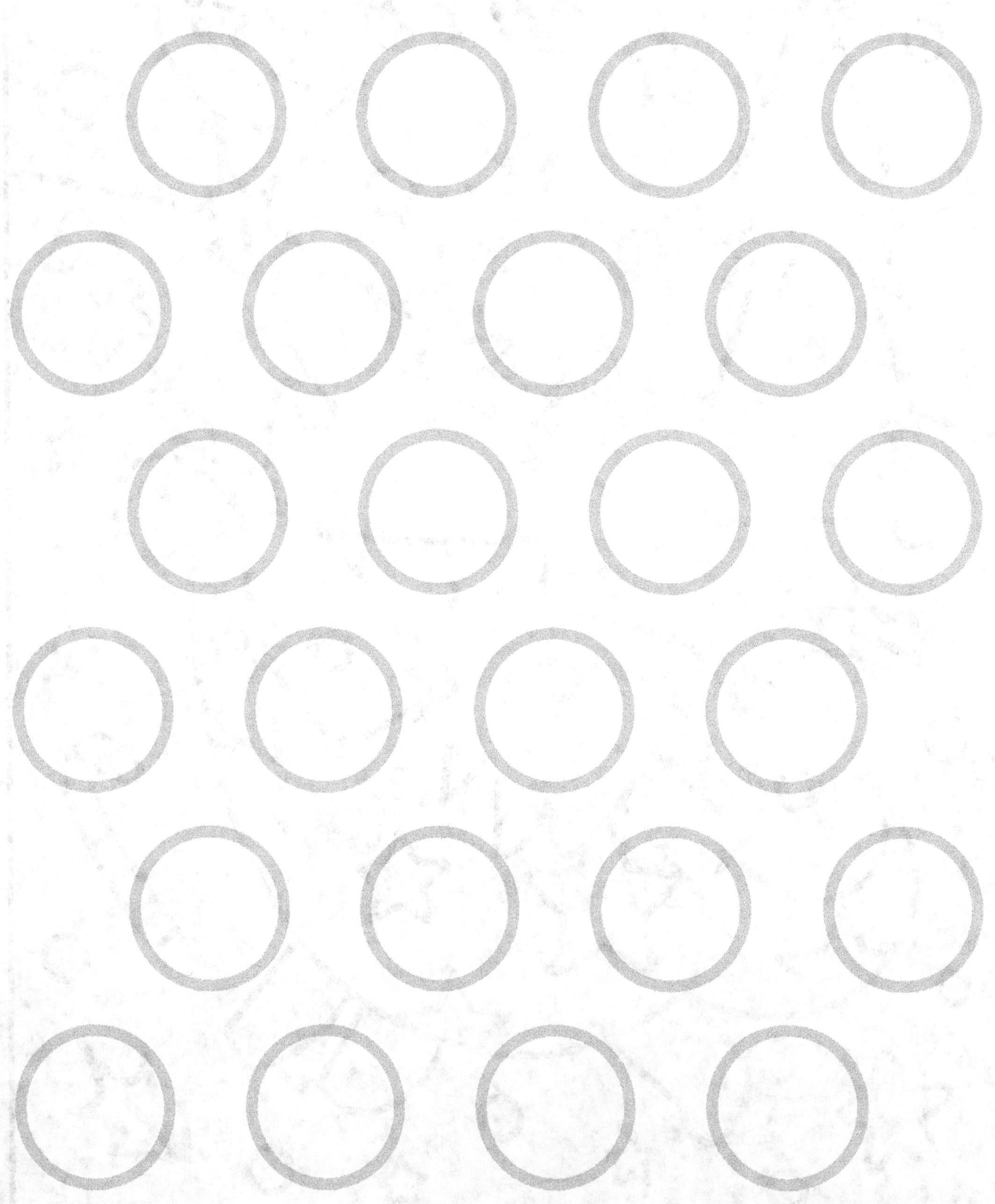

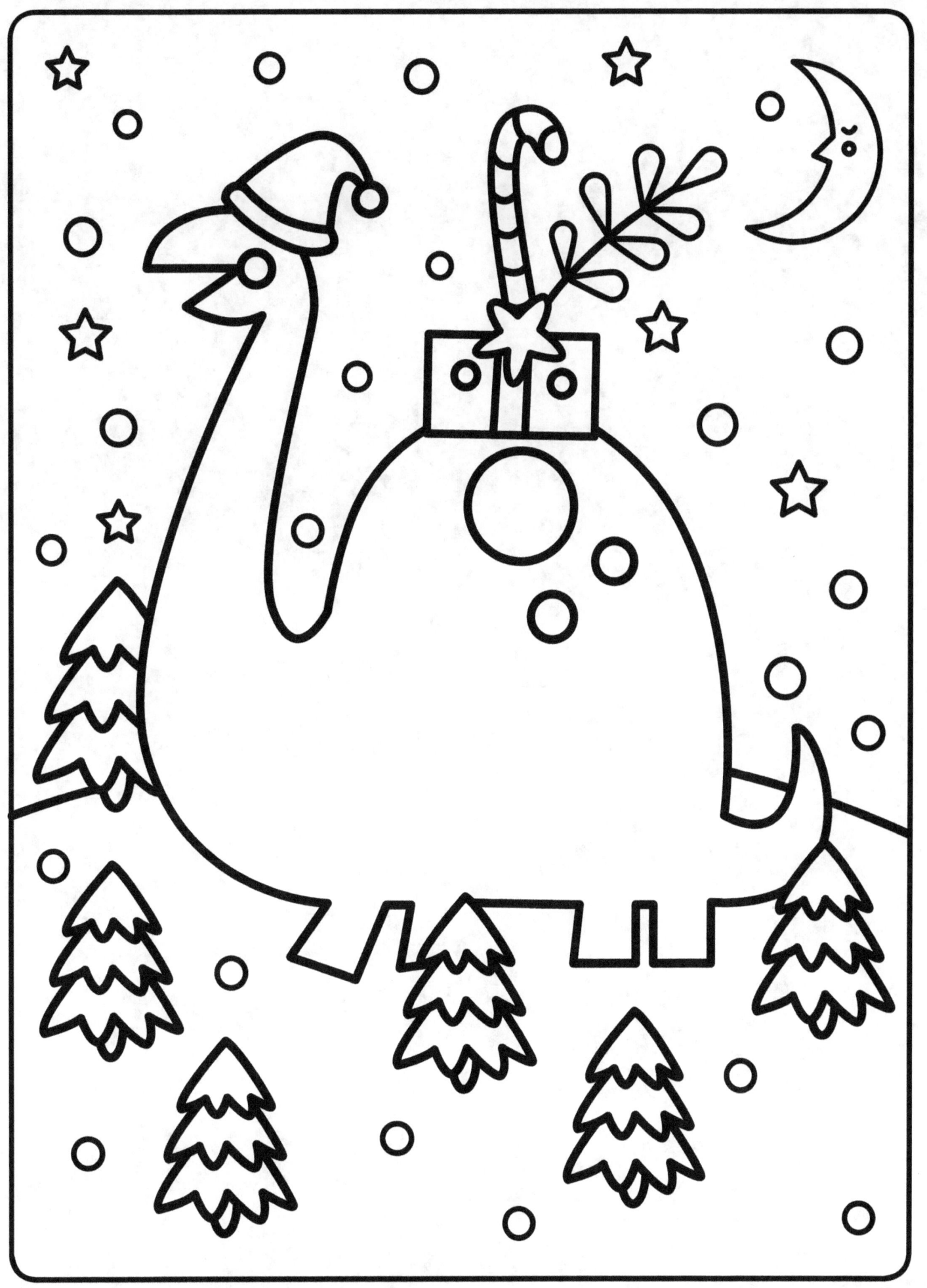

COLOR CHARTS TEST

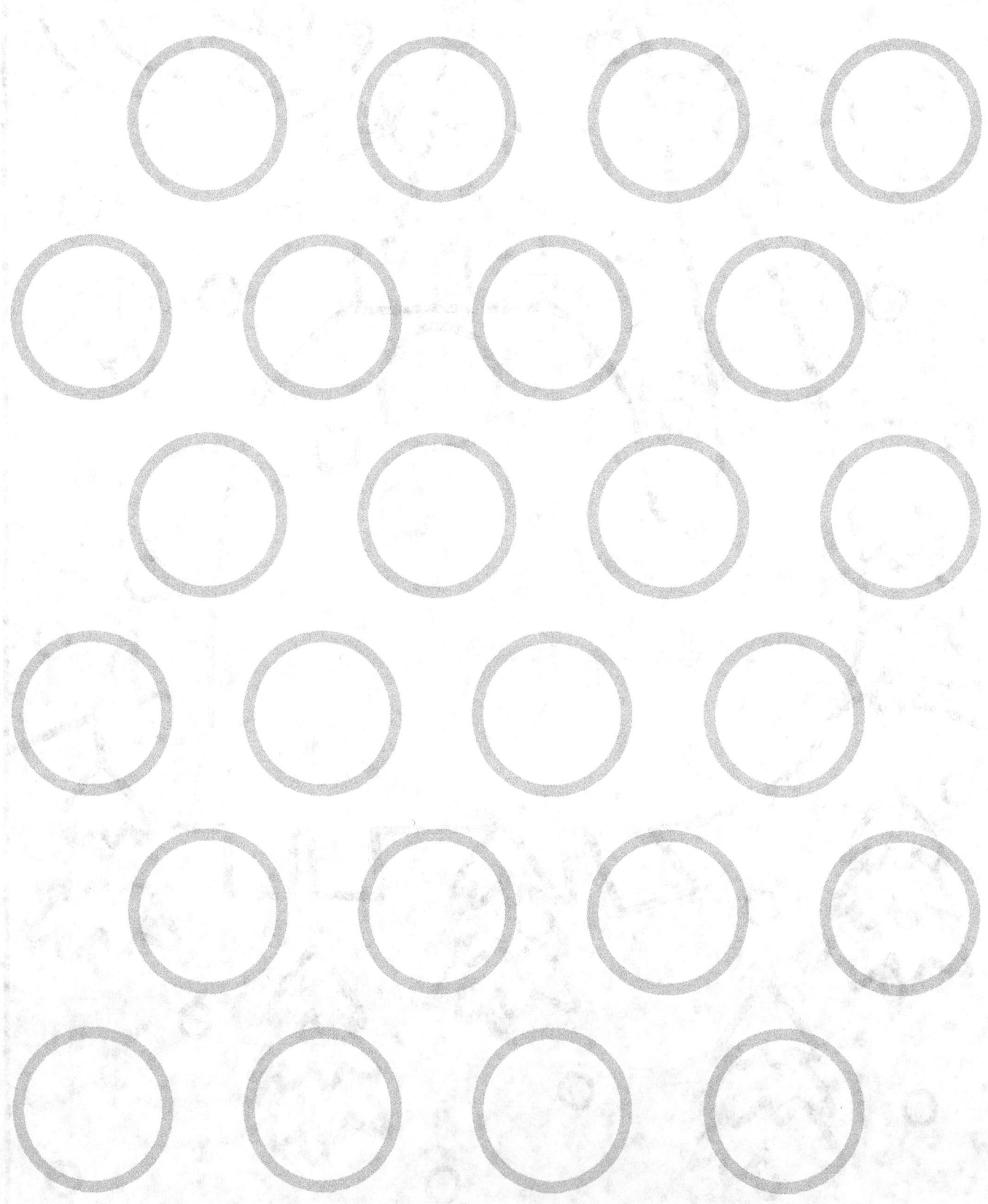

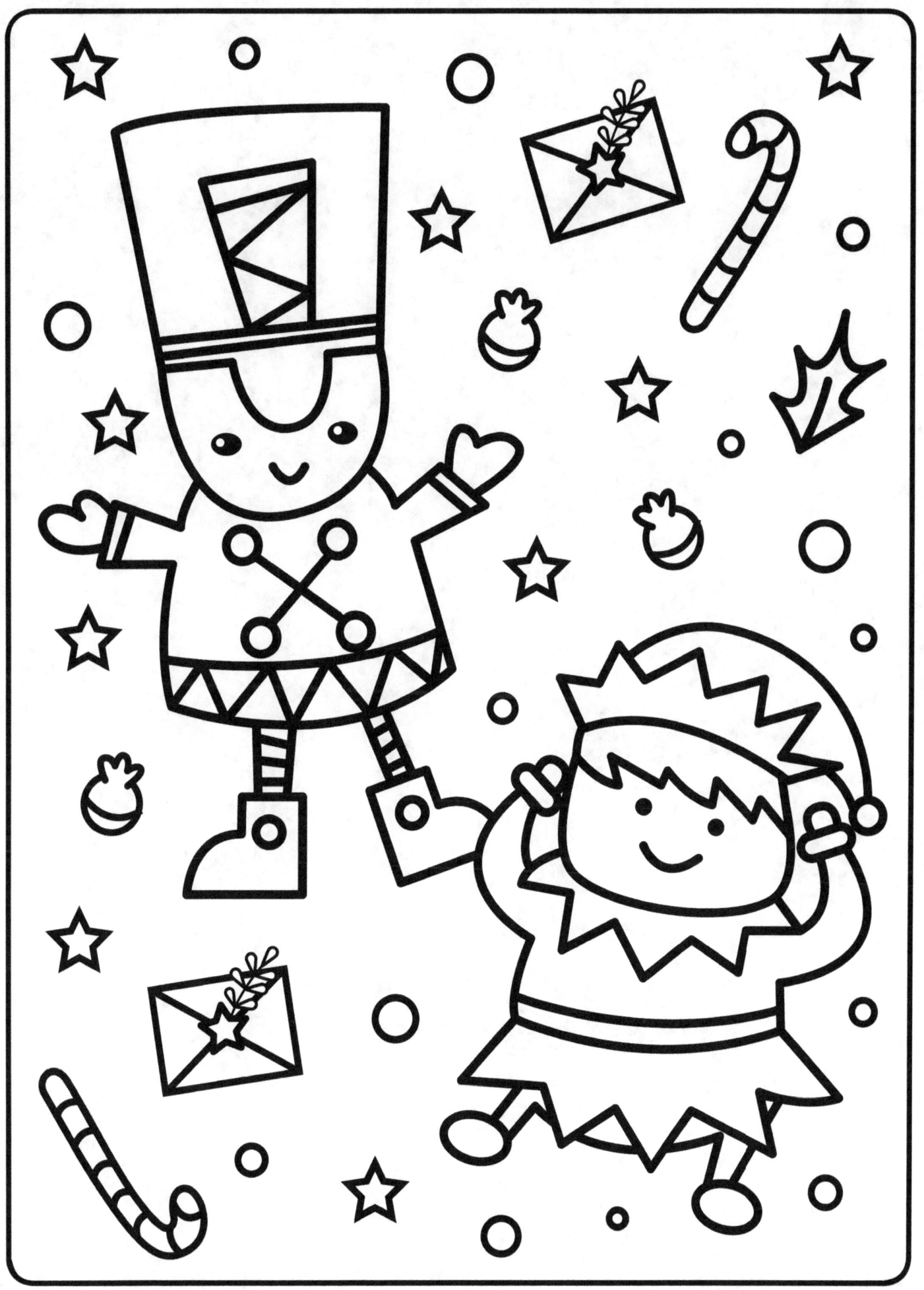

COLOR CHARTS TEST

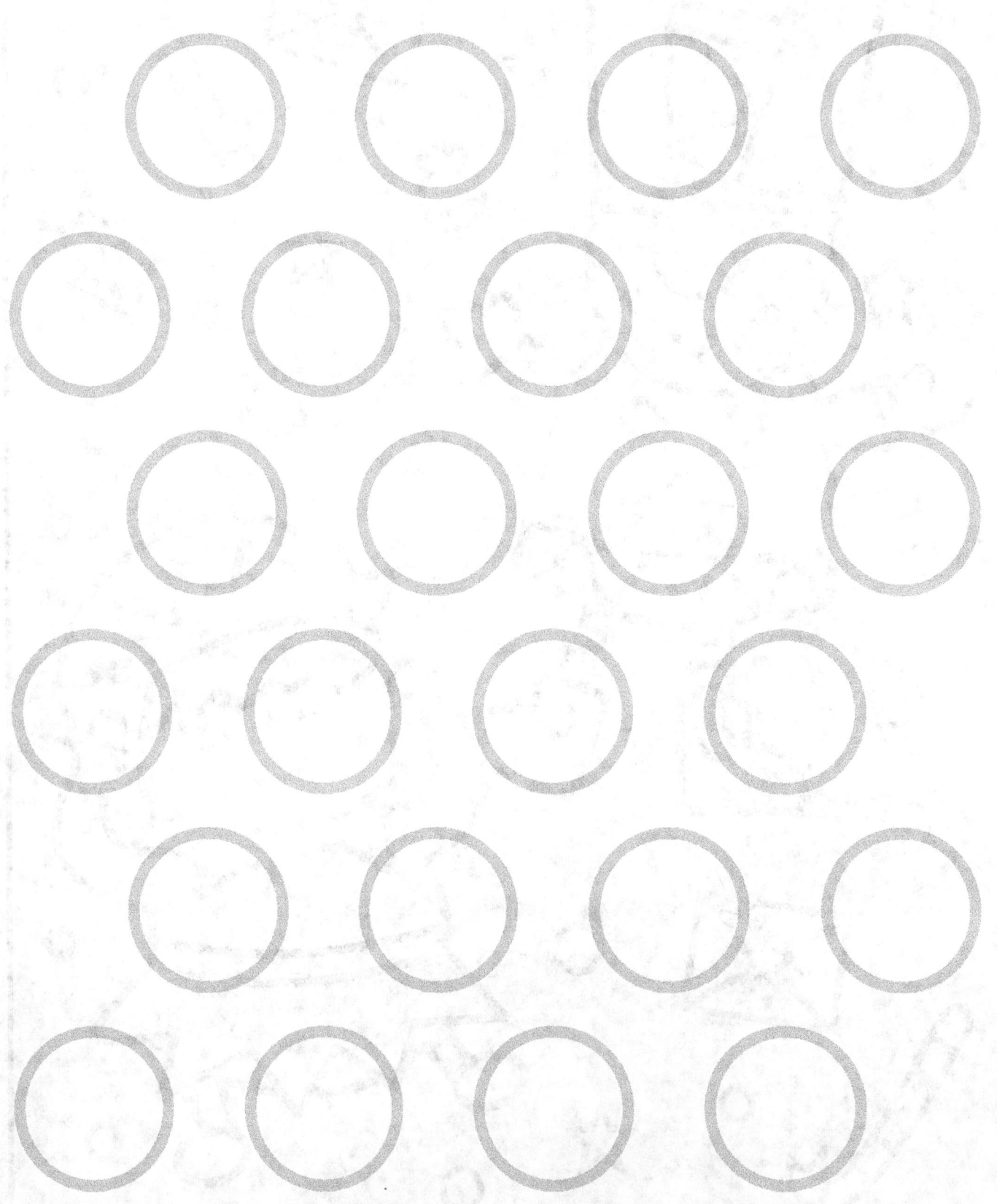

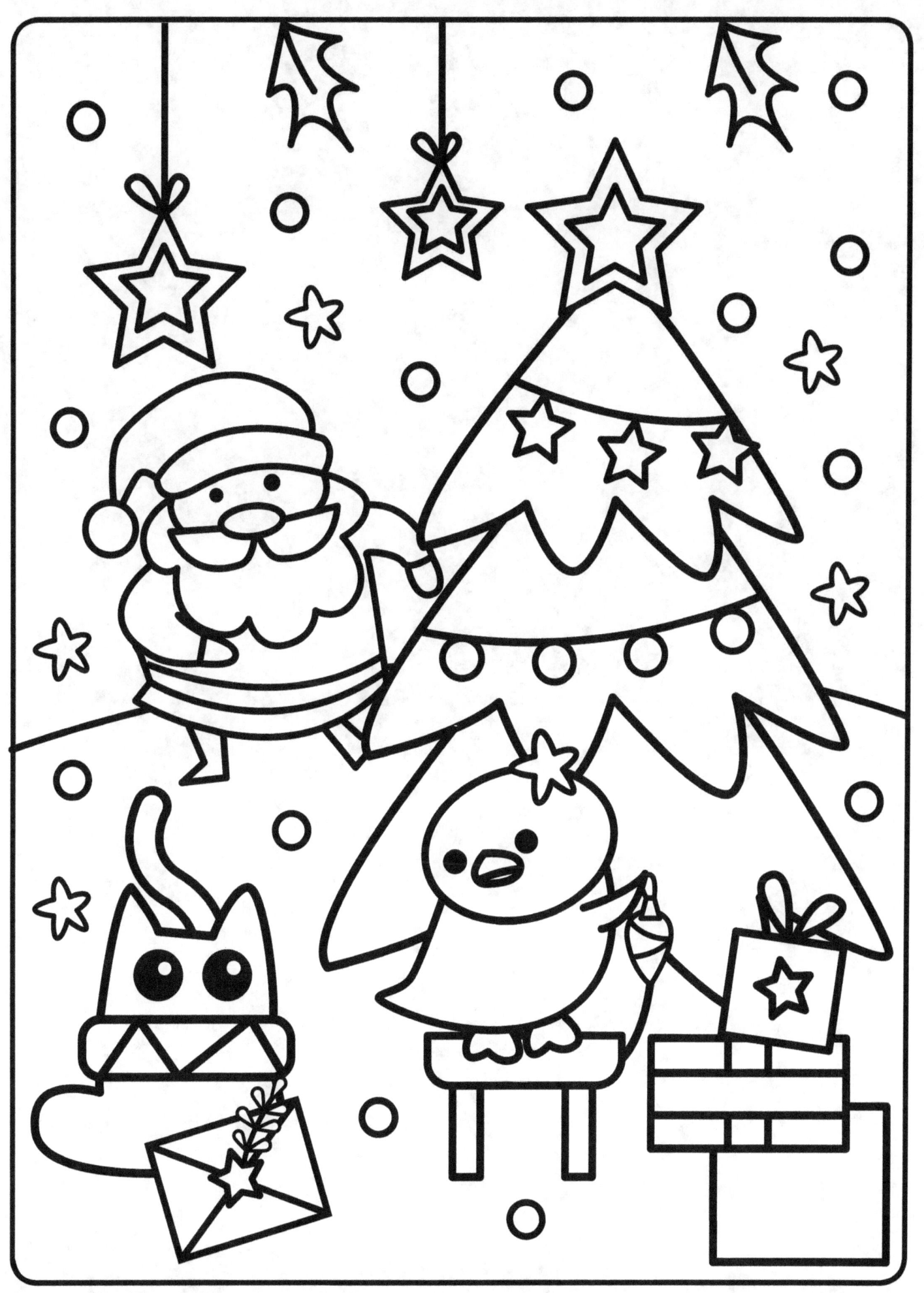

COLOR CHARTS TEST

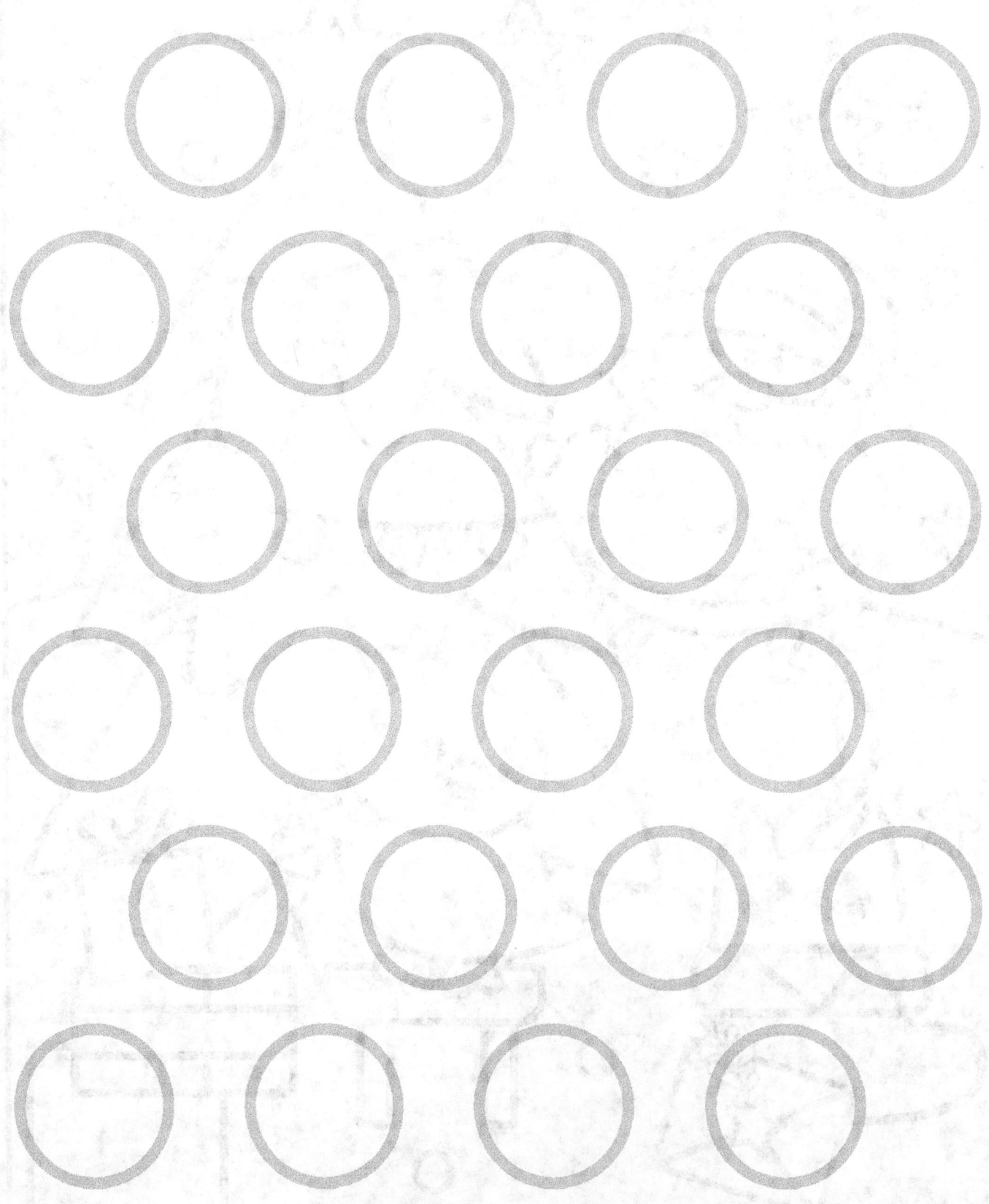

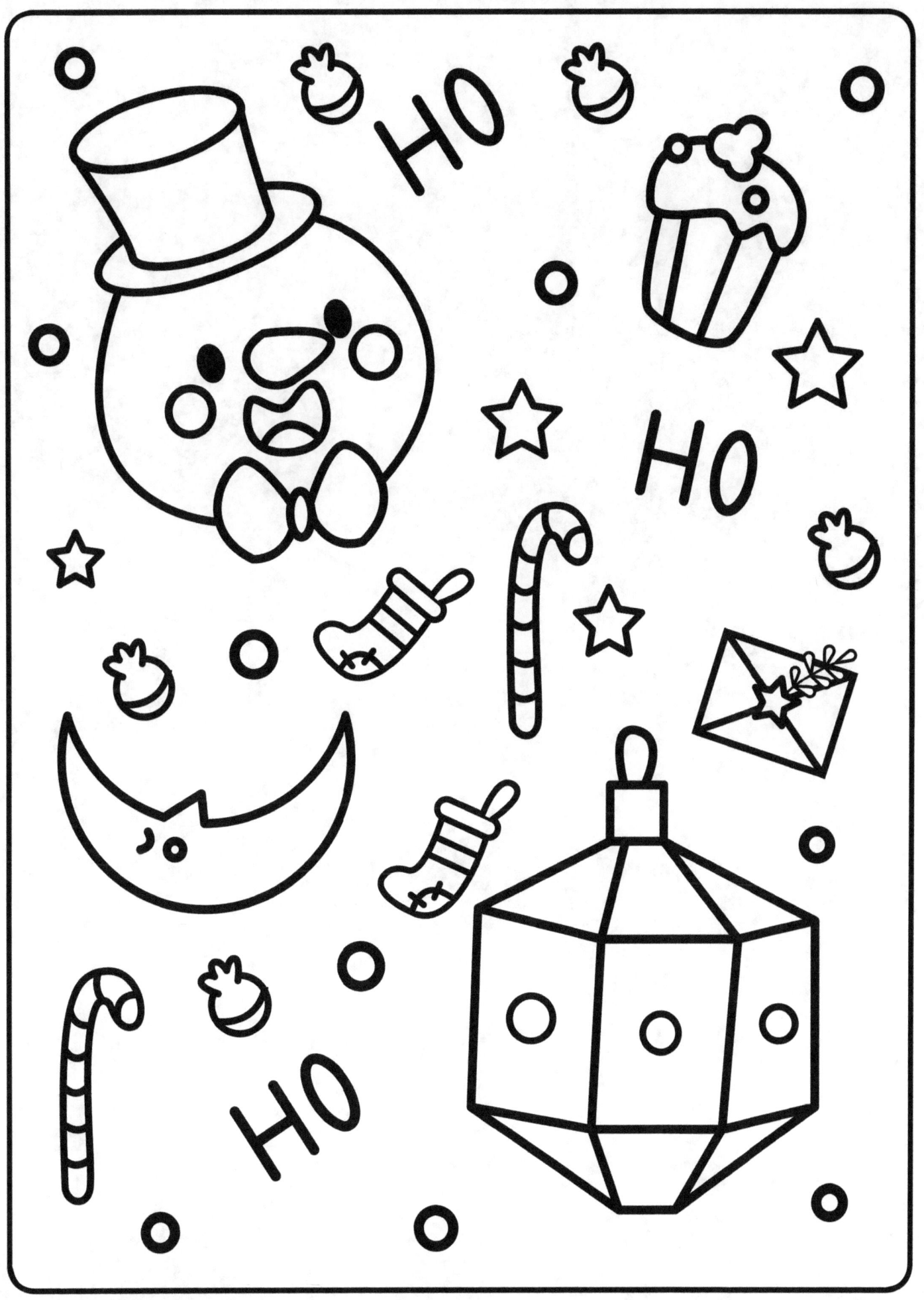

COLOR CHARTS TEST

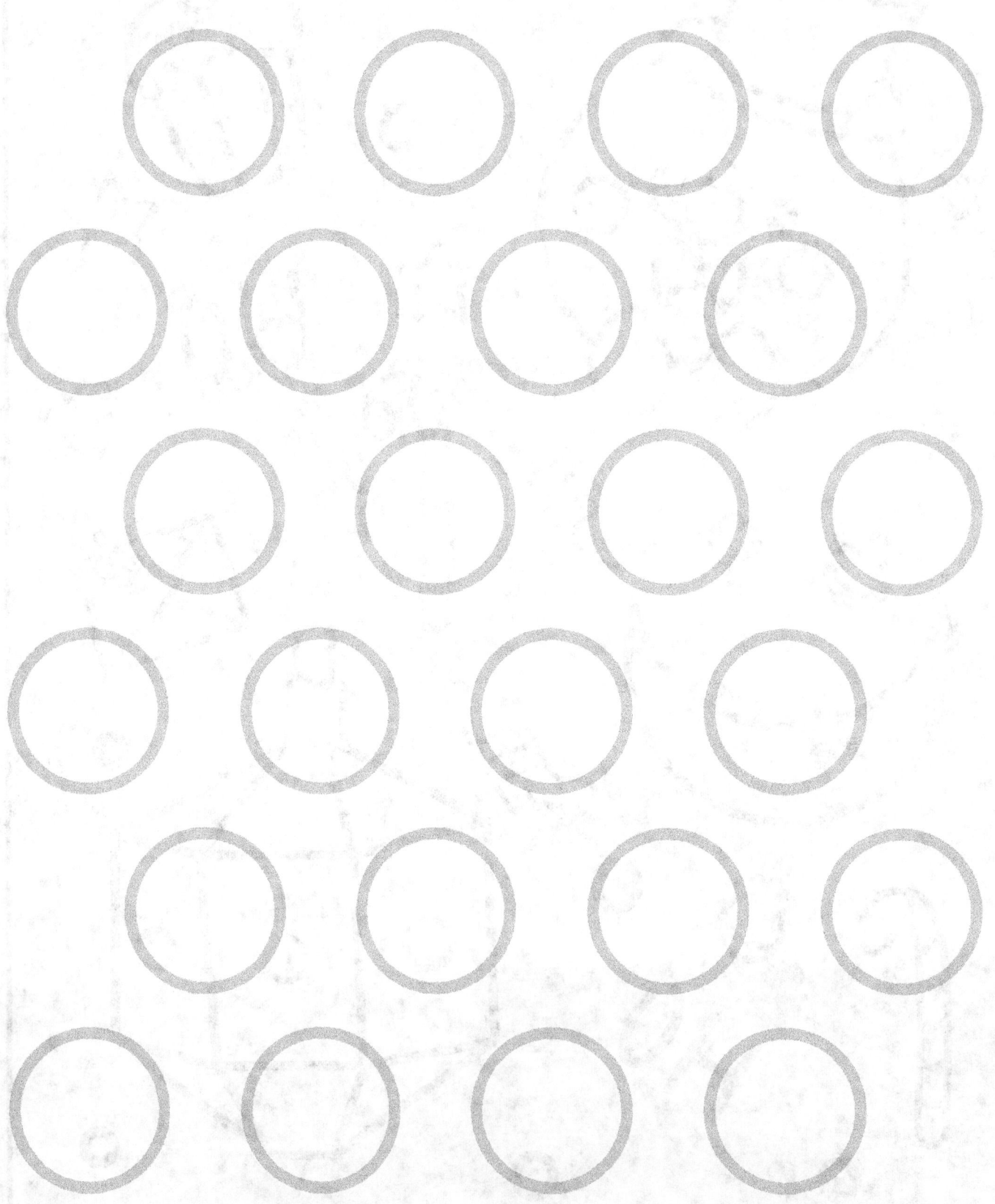

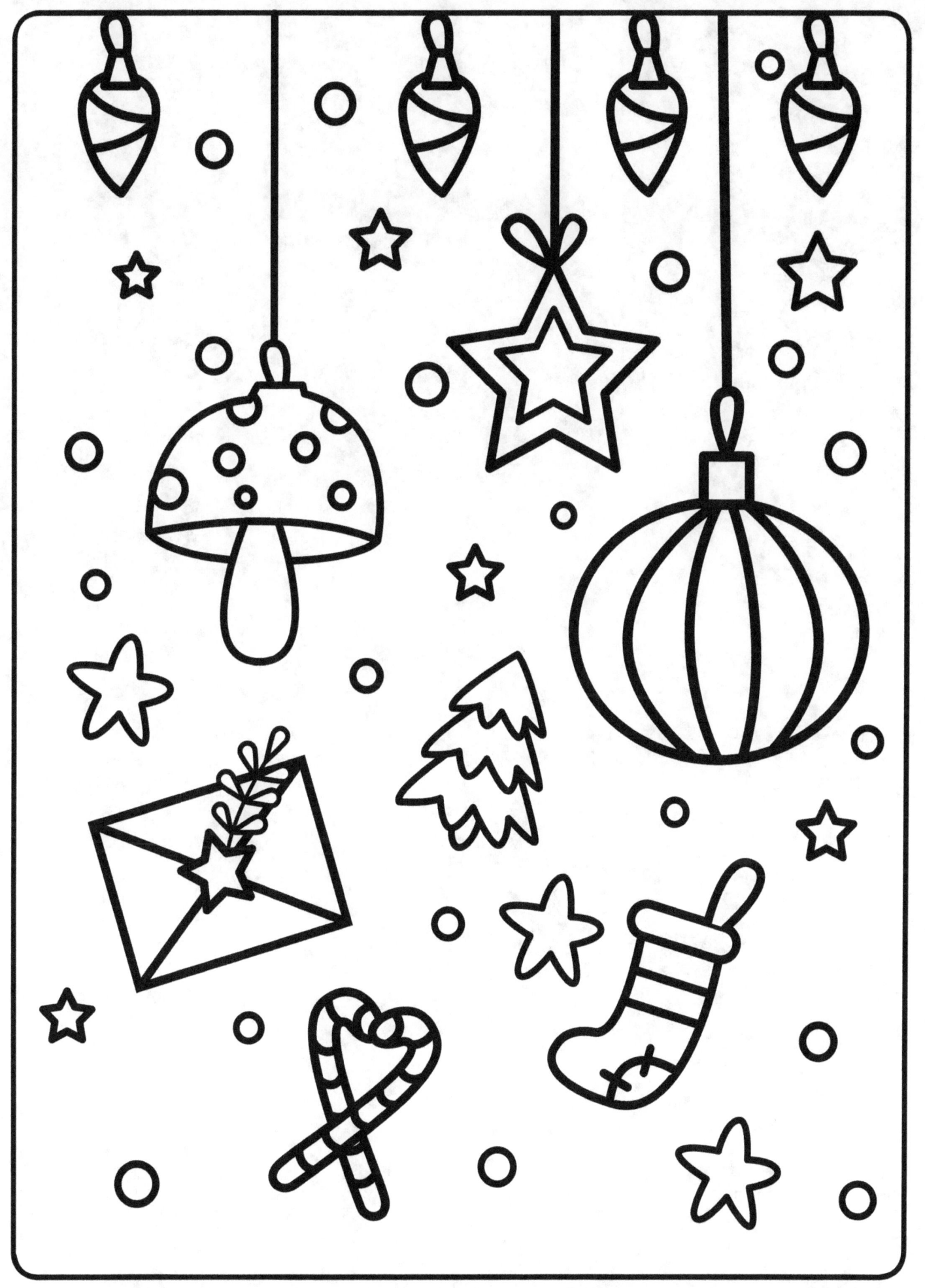

COLOR CHARTS TEST

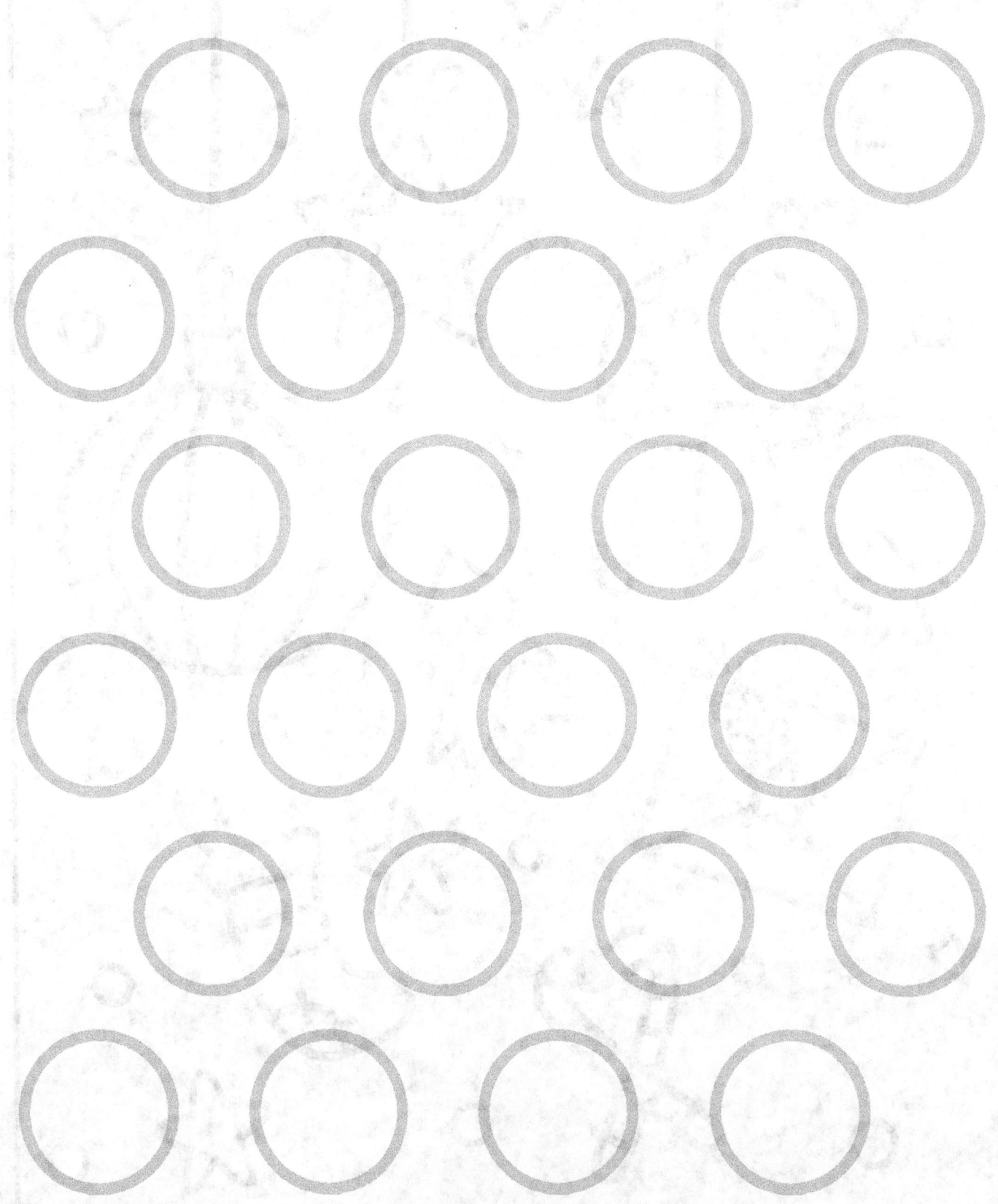

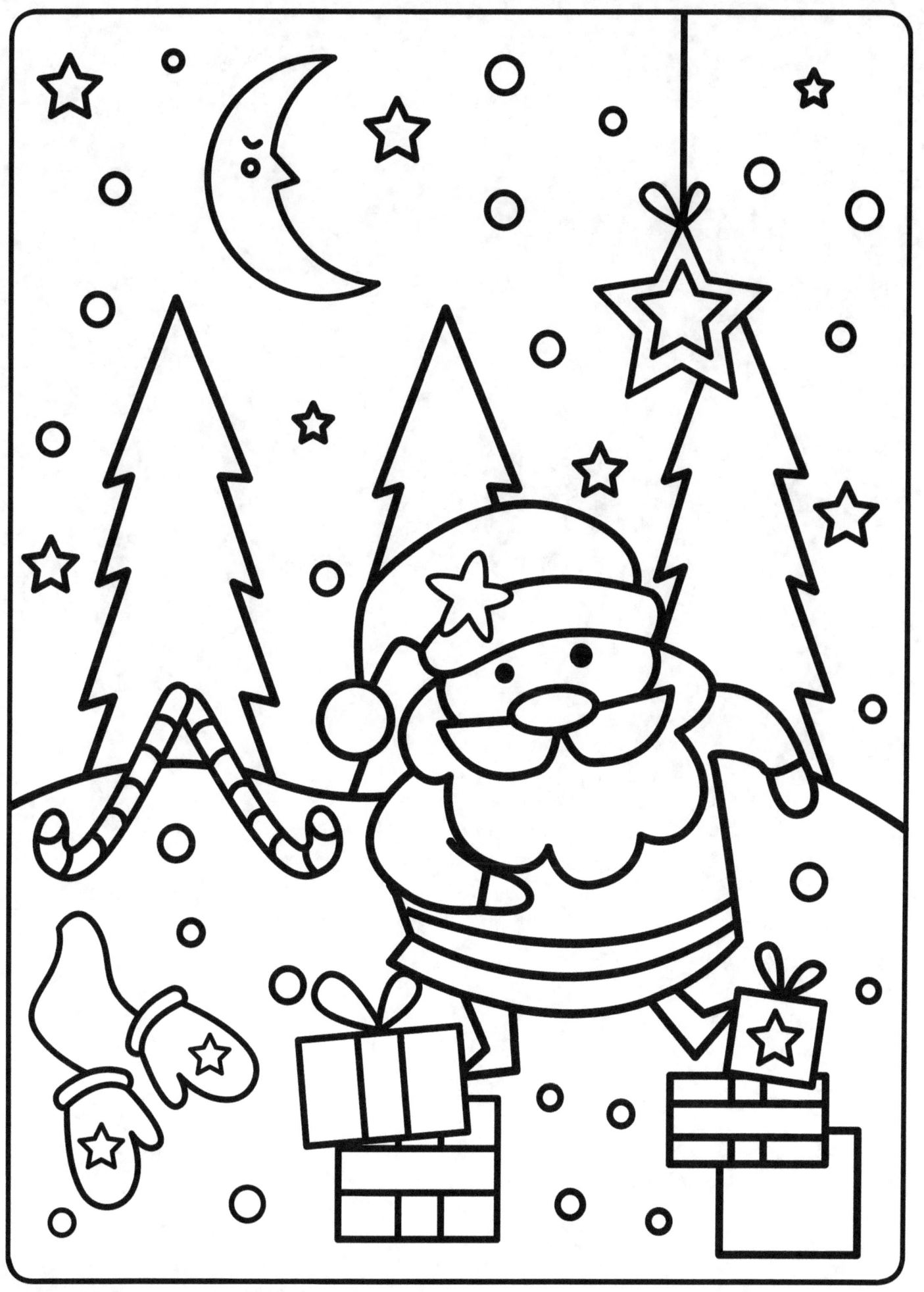

COLOR CHARTS TEST

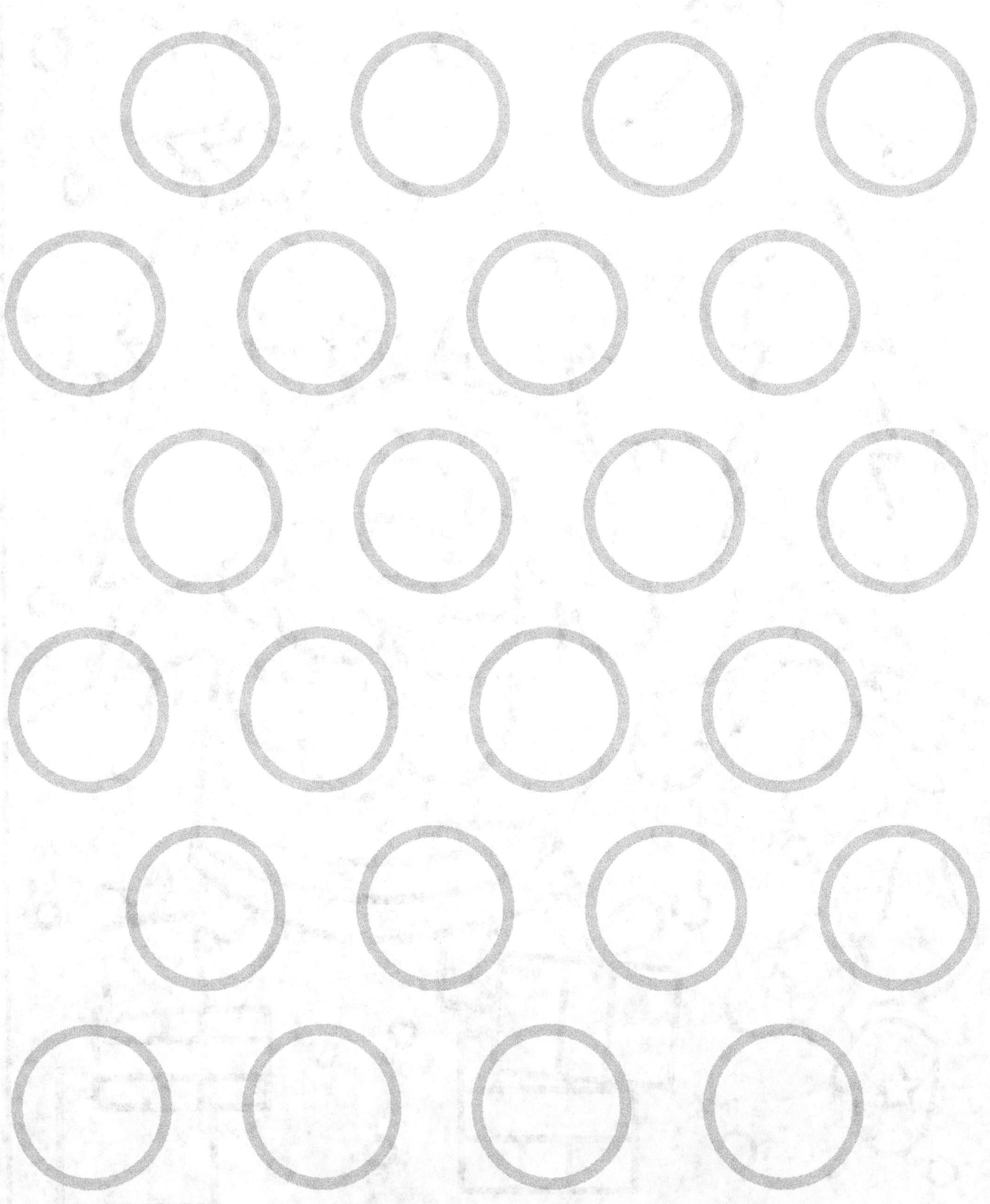

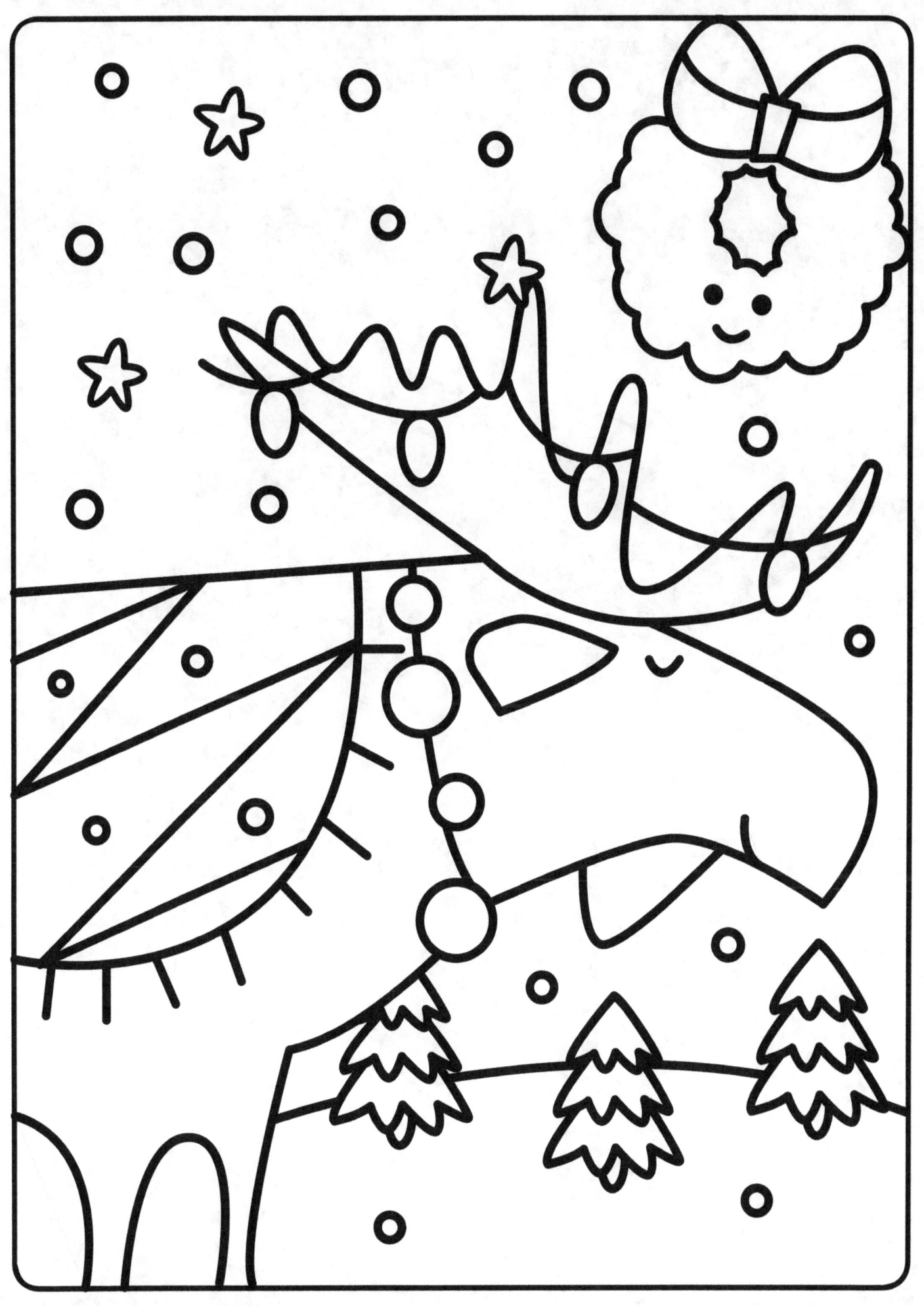

COLOR CHARTS TEST

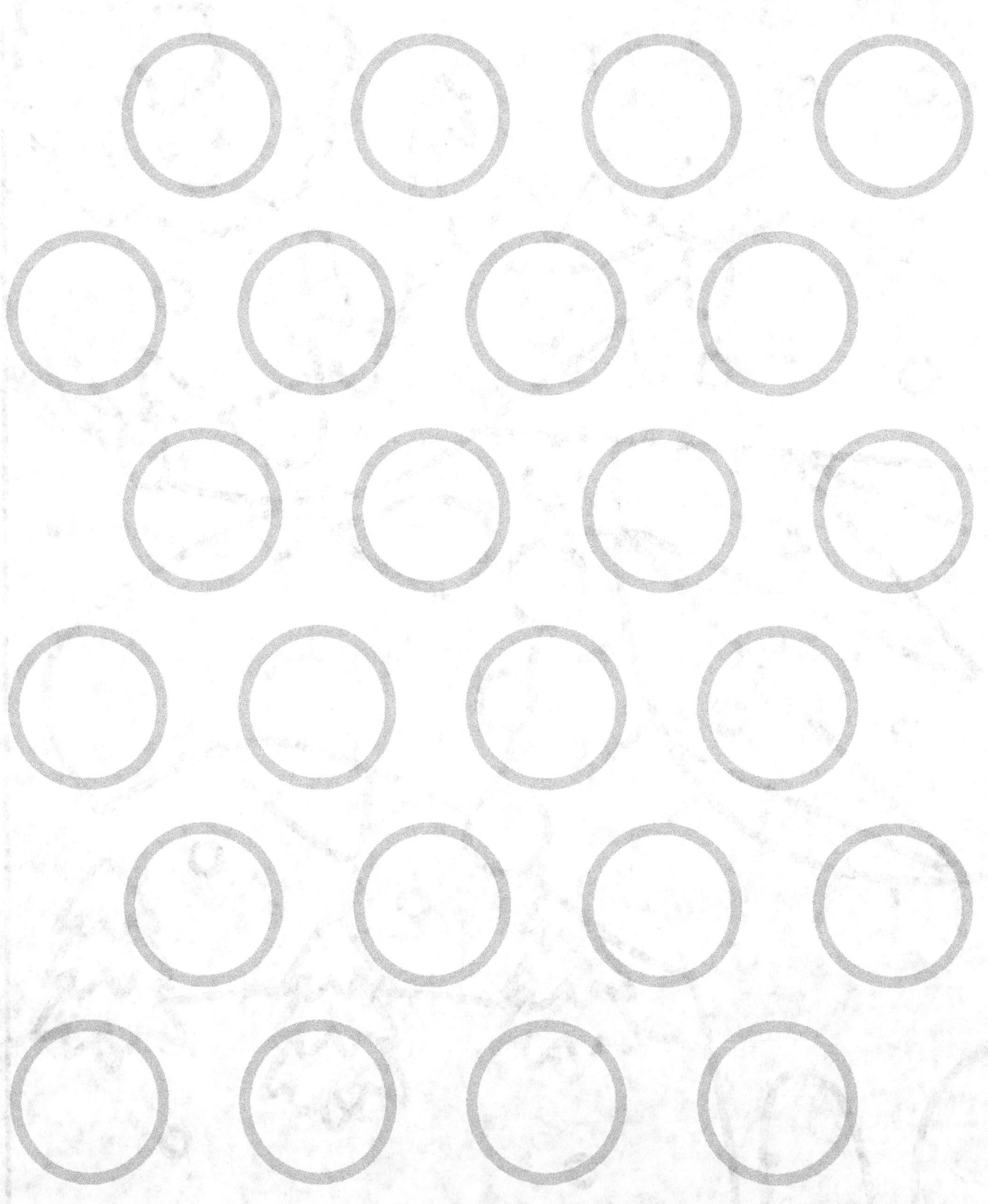

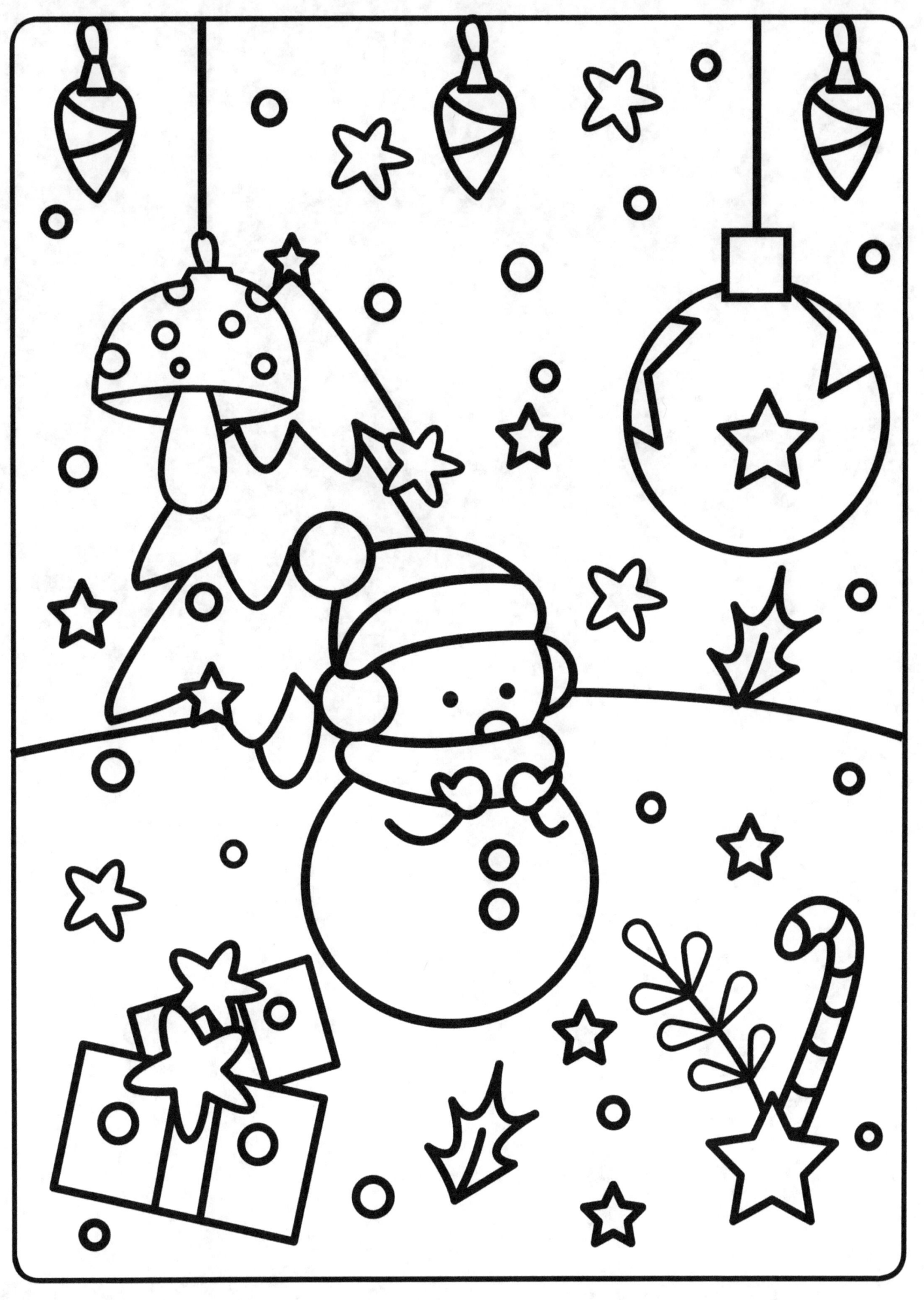

COLOR CHARTS TEST

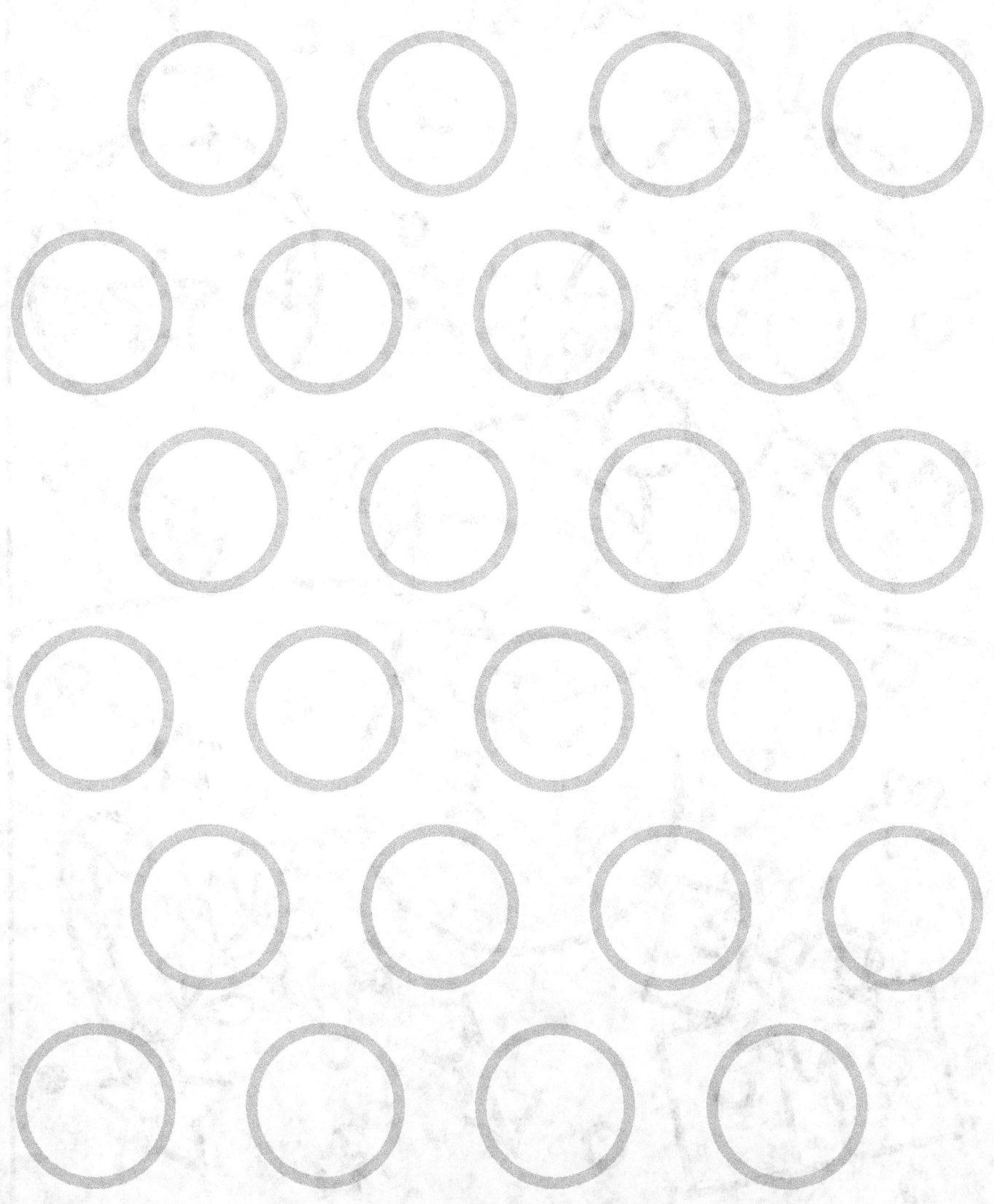

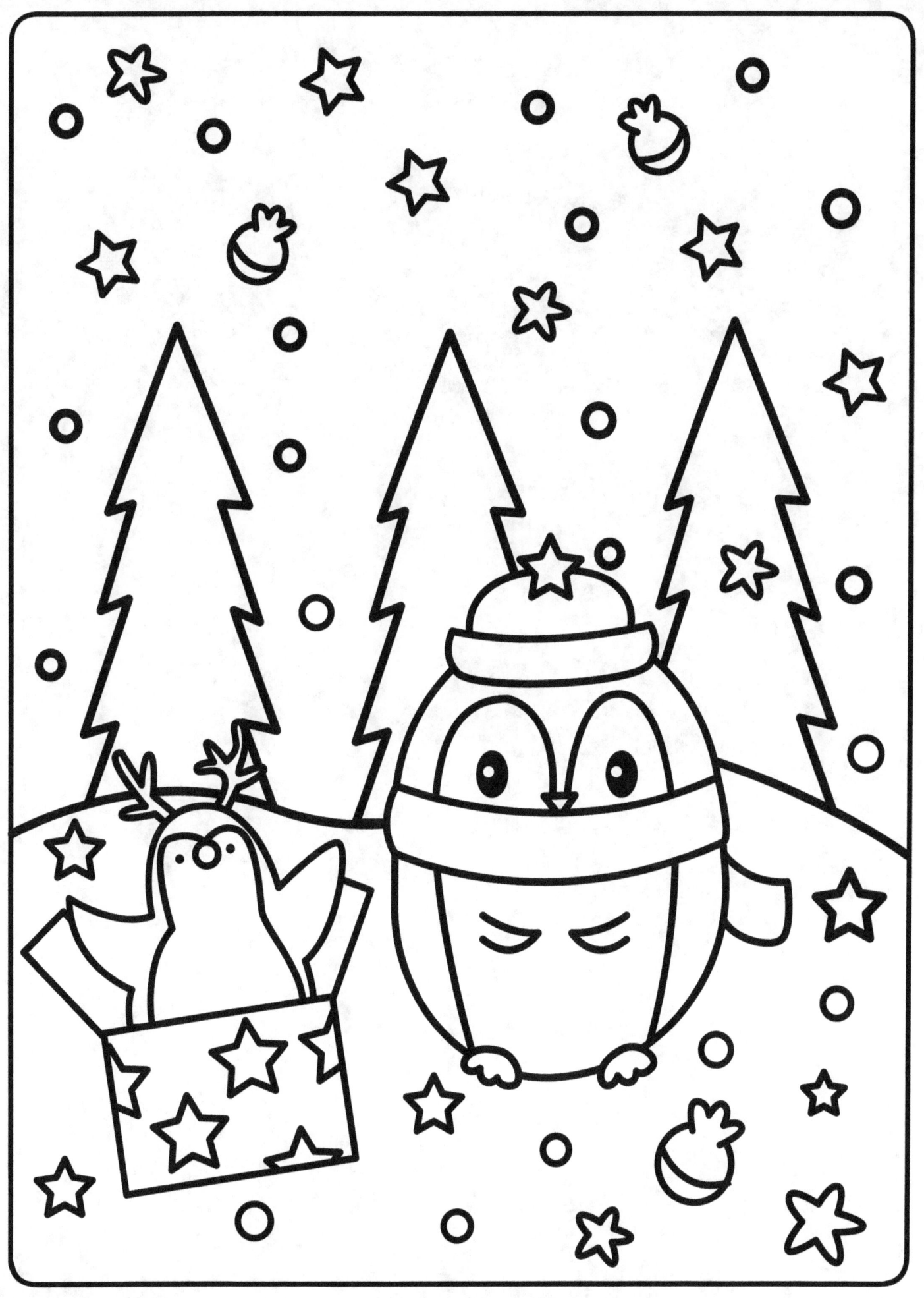

COLOR CHARTS TEST

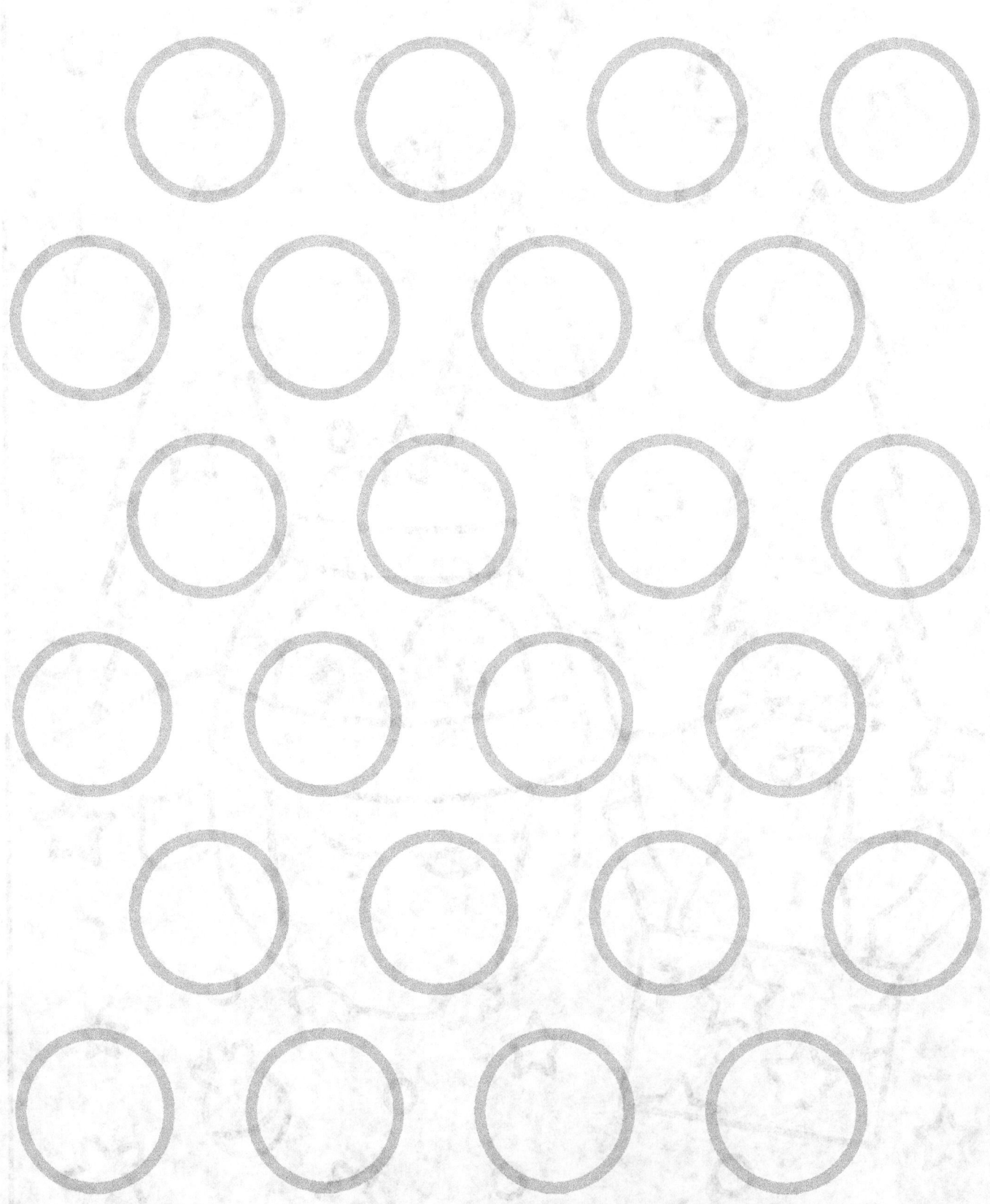

COLOR CHARTS TEST

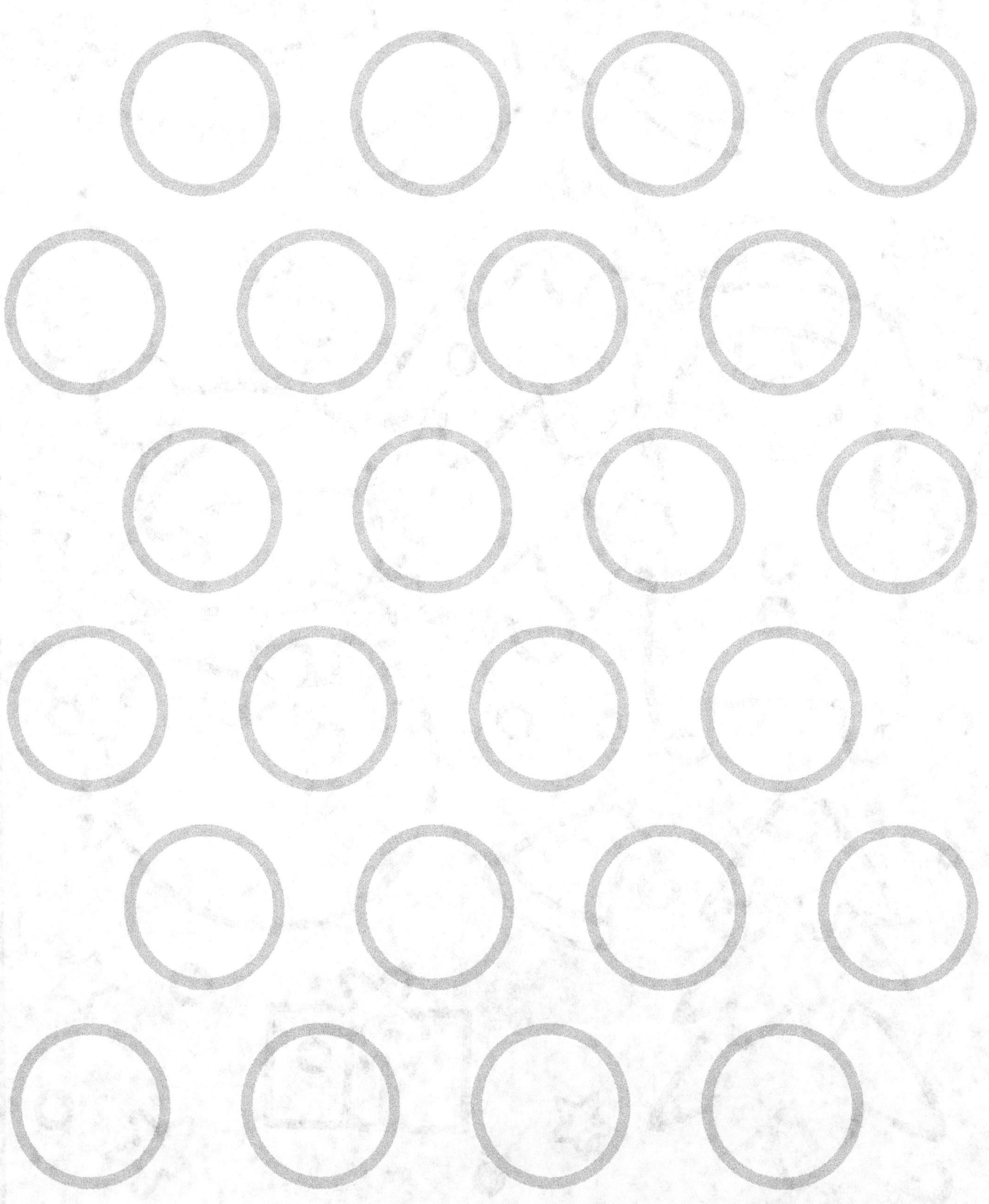

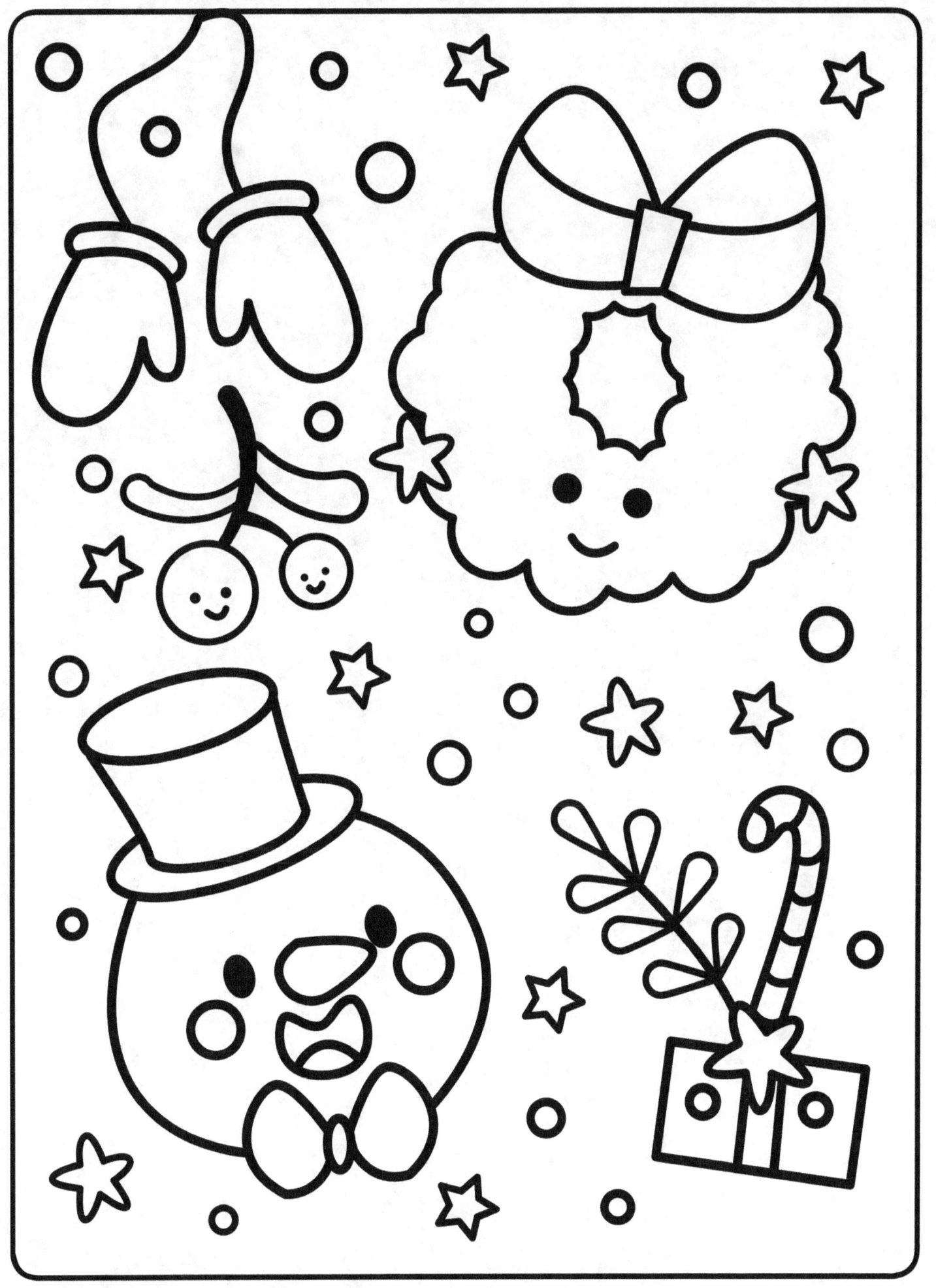

COLOR CHARTS TEST

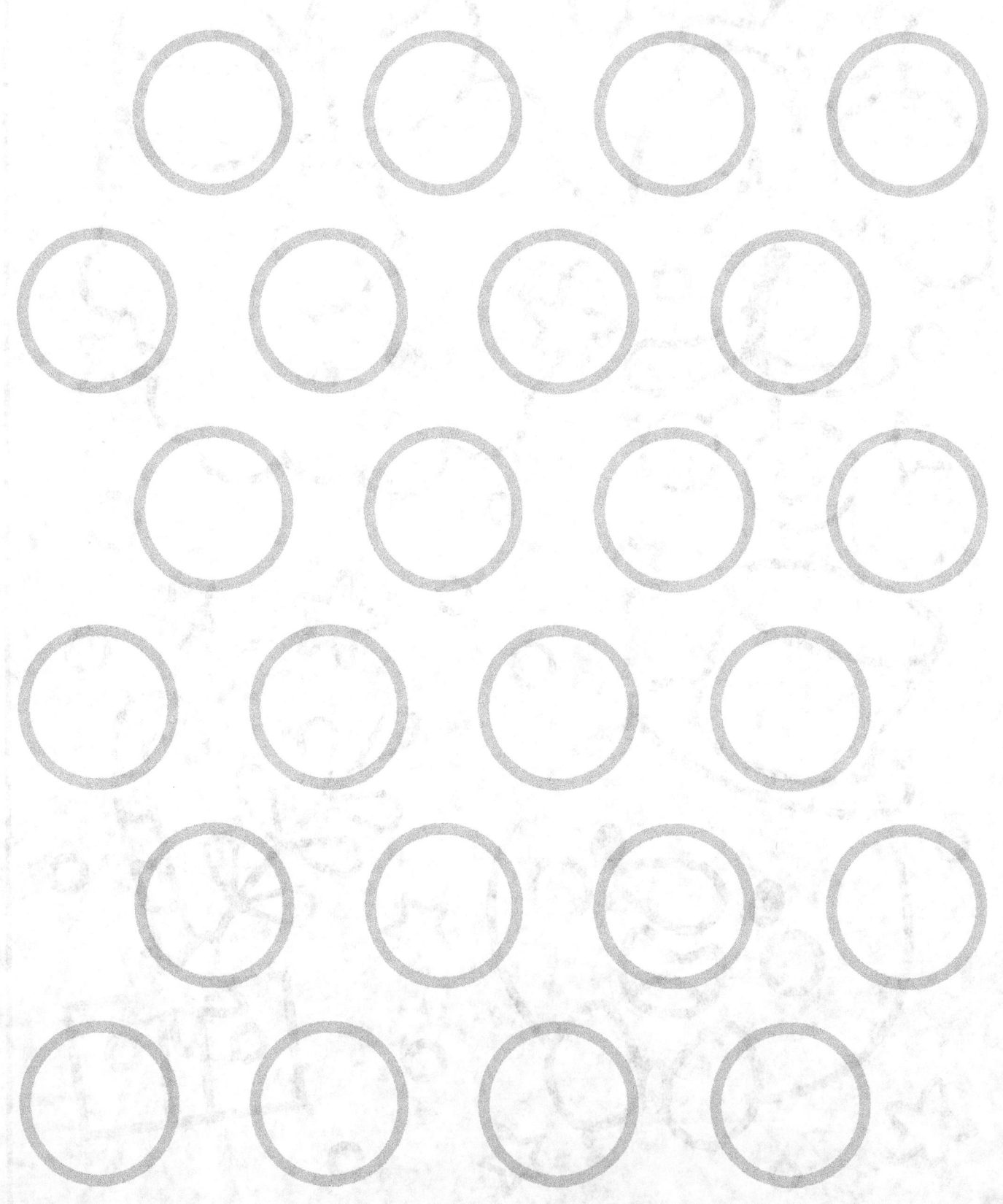

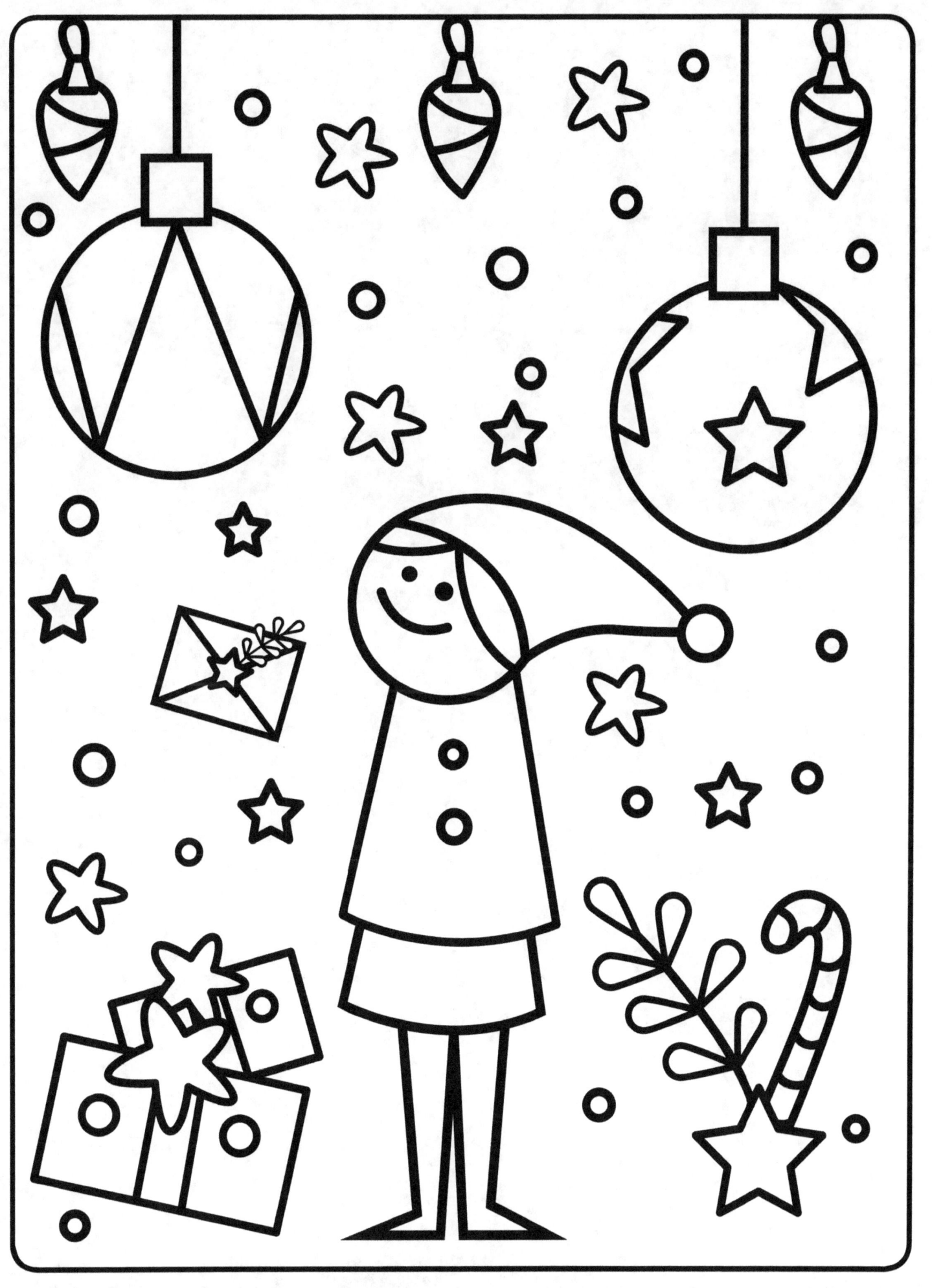

COLOR CHARTS TEST

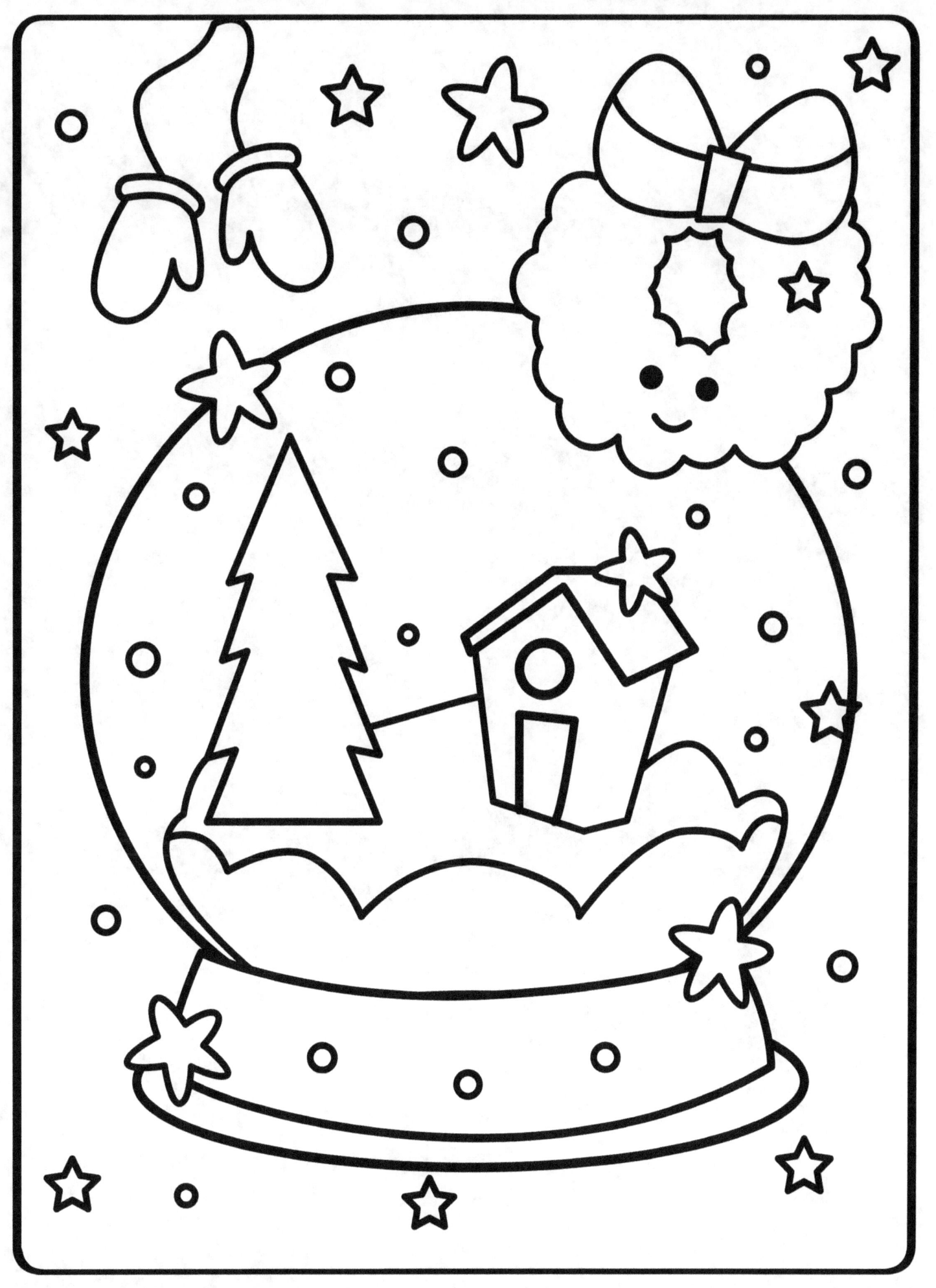

COLOR CHARTS TEST

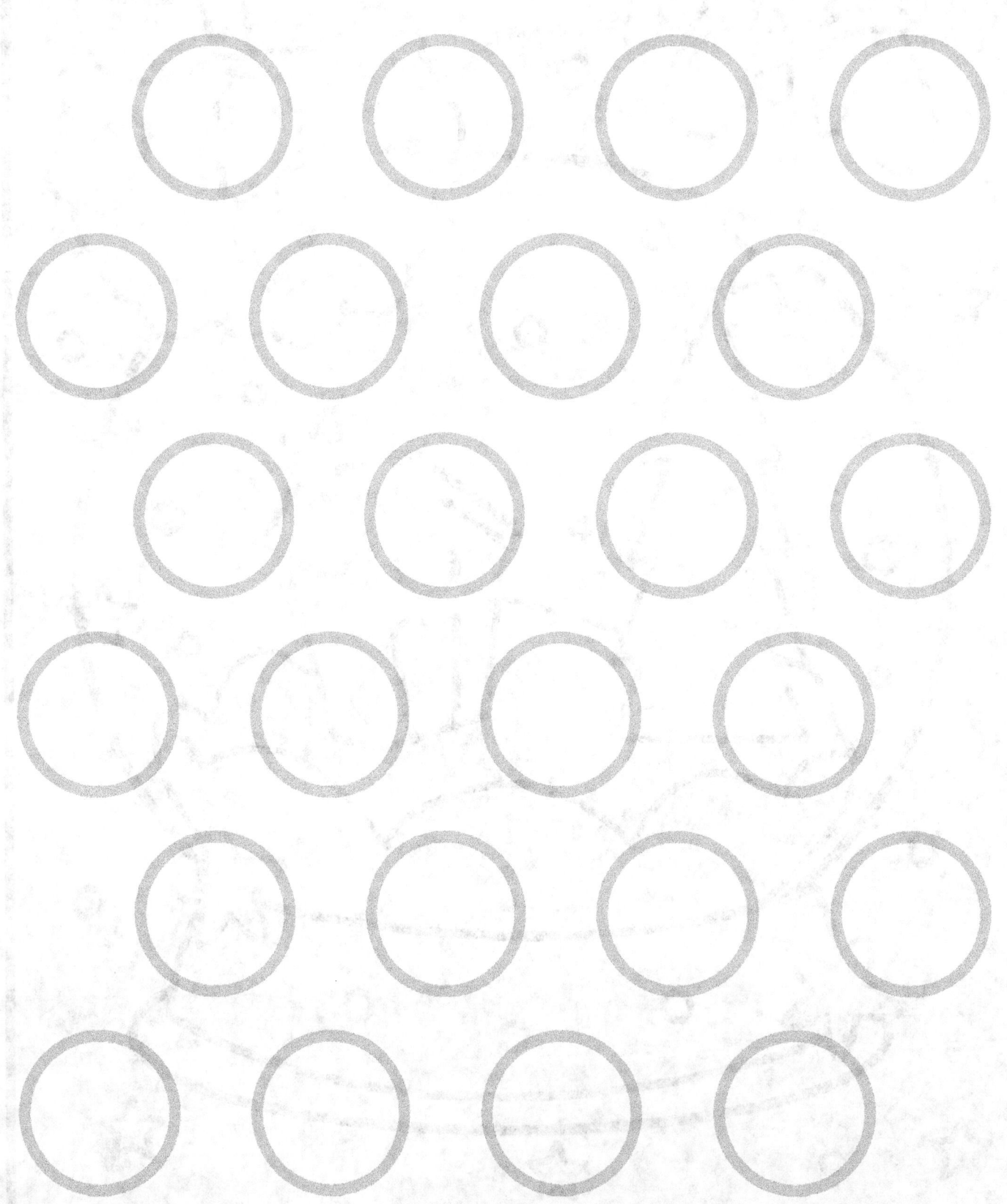

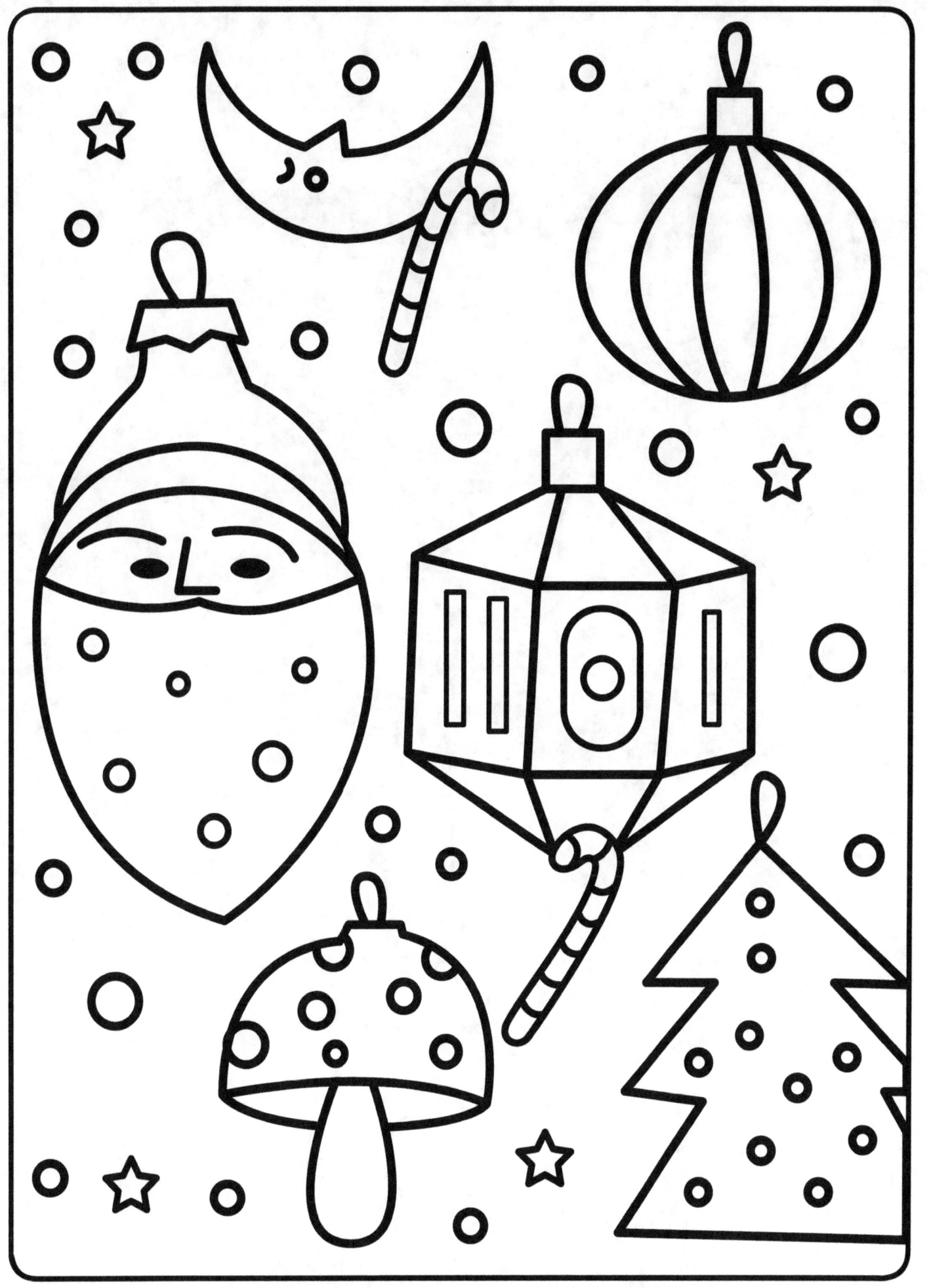

COLOR CHARTS TEST

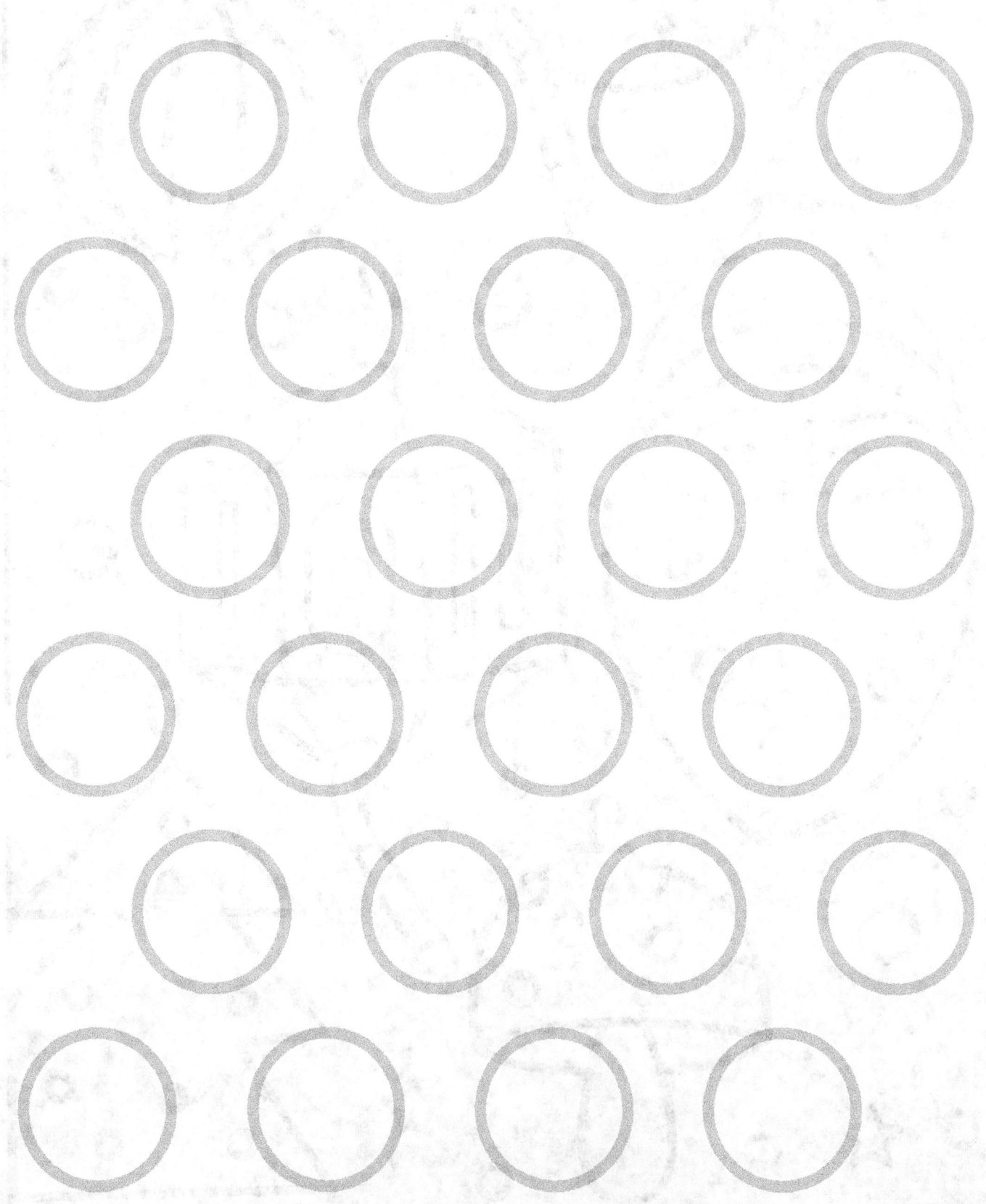

COLOR CHARTS TEST

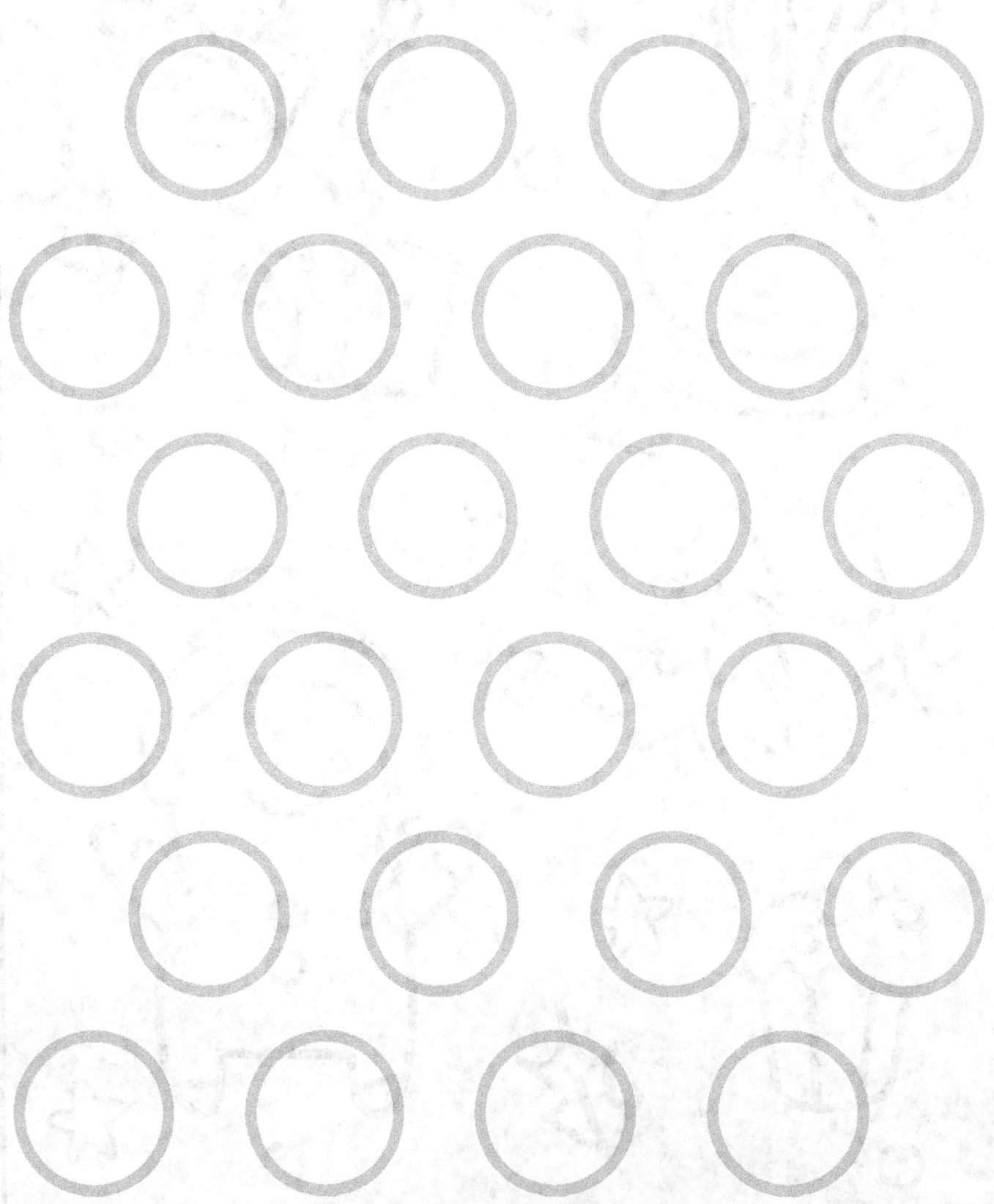

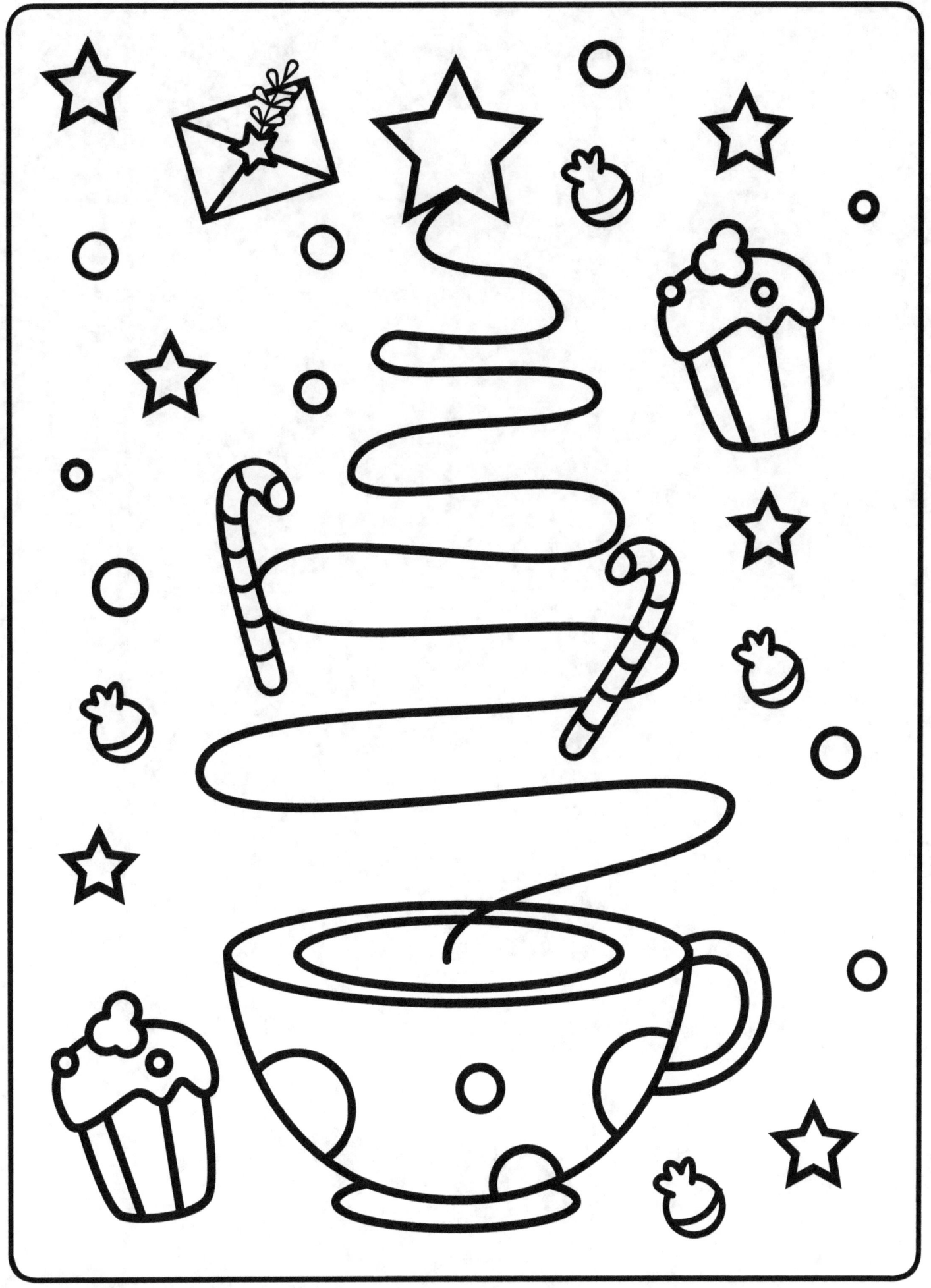

COLOR CHARTS TEST

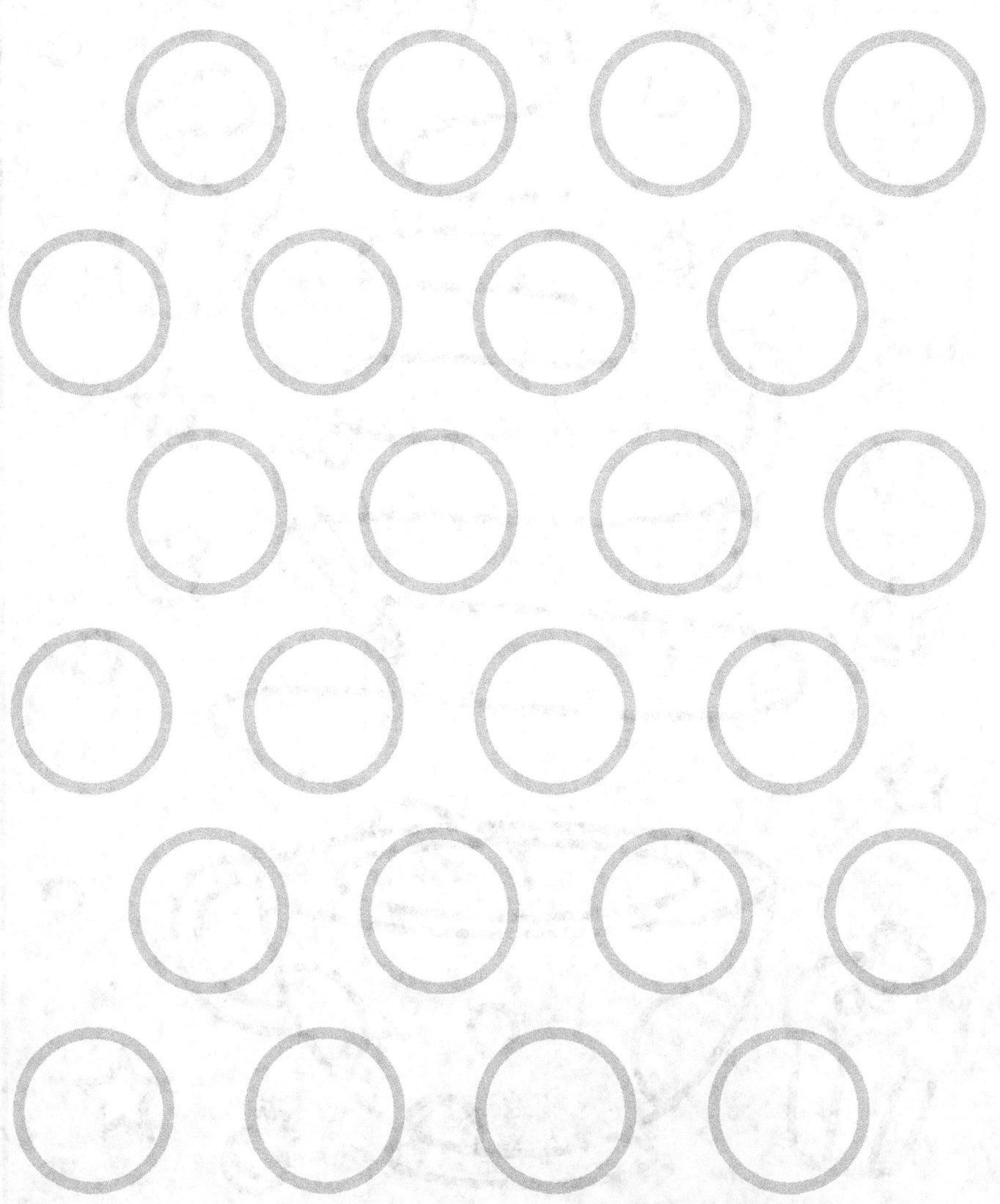

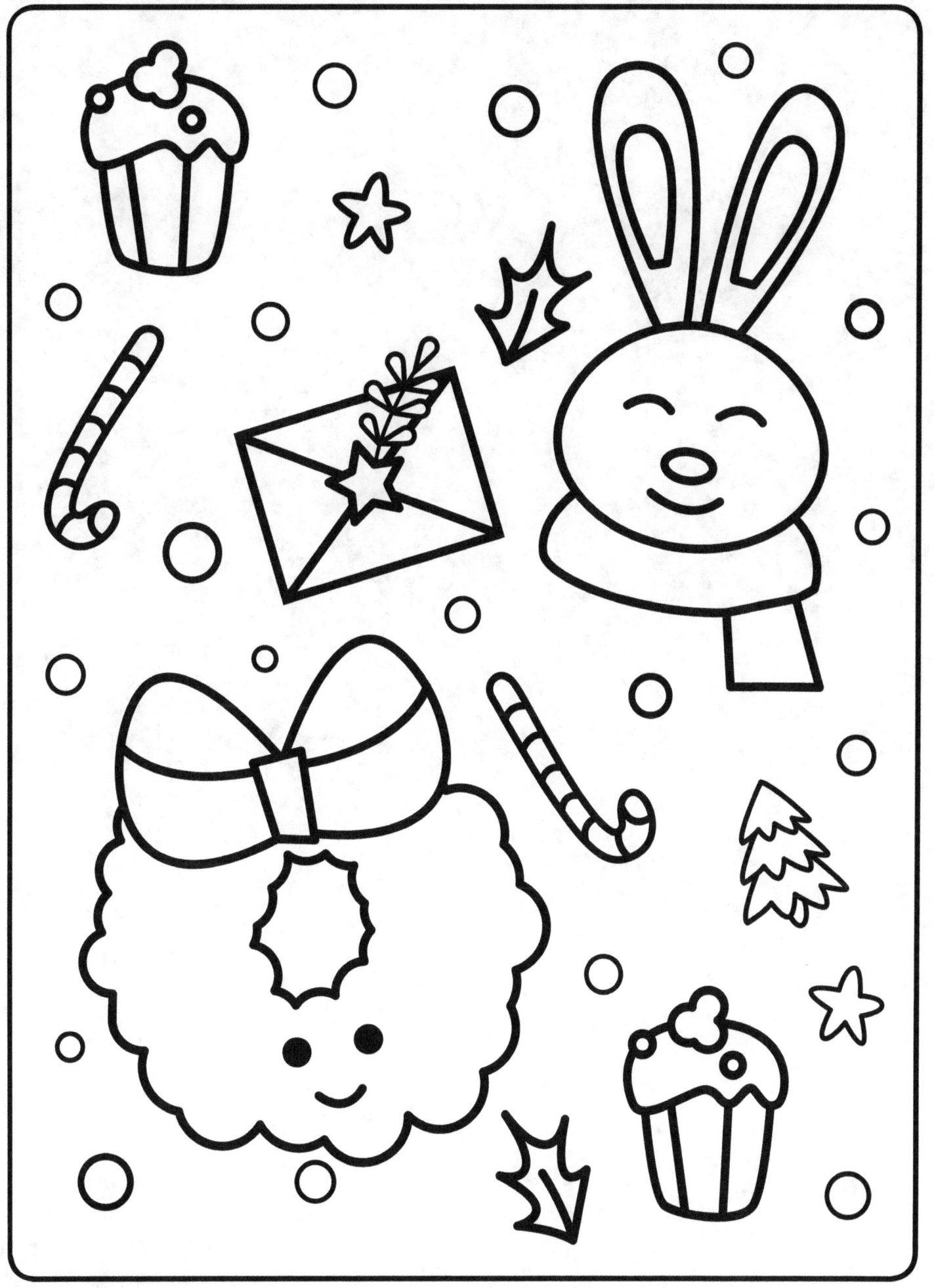

COLOR CHARTS TEST

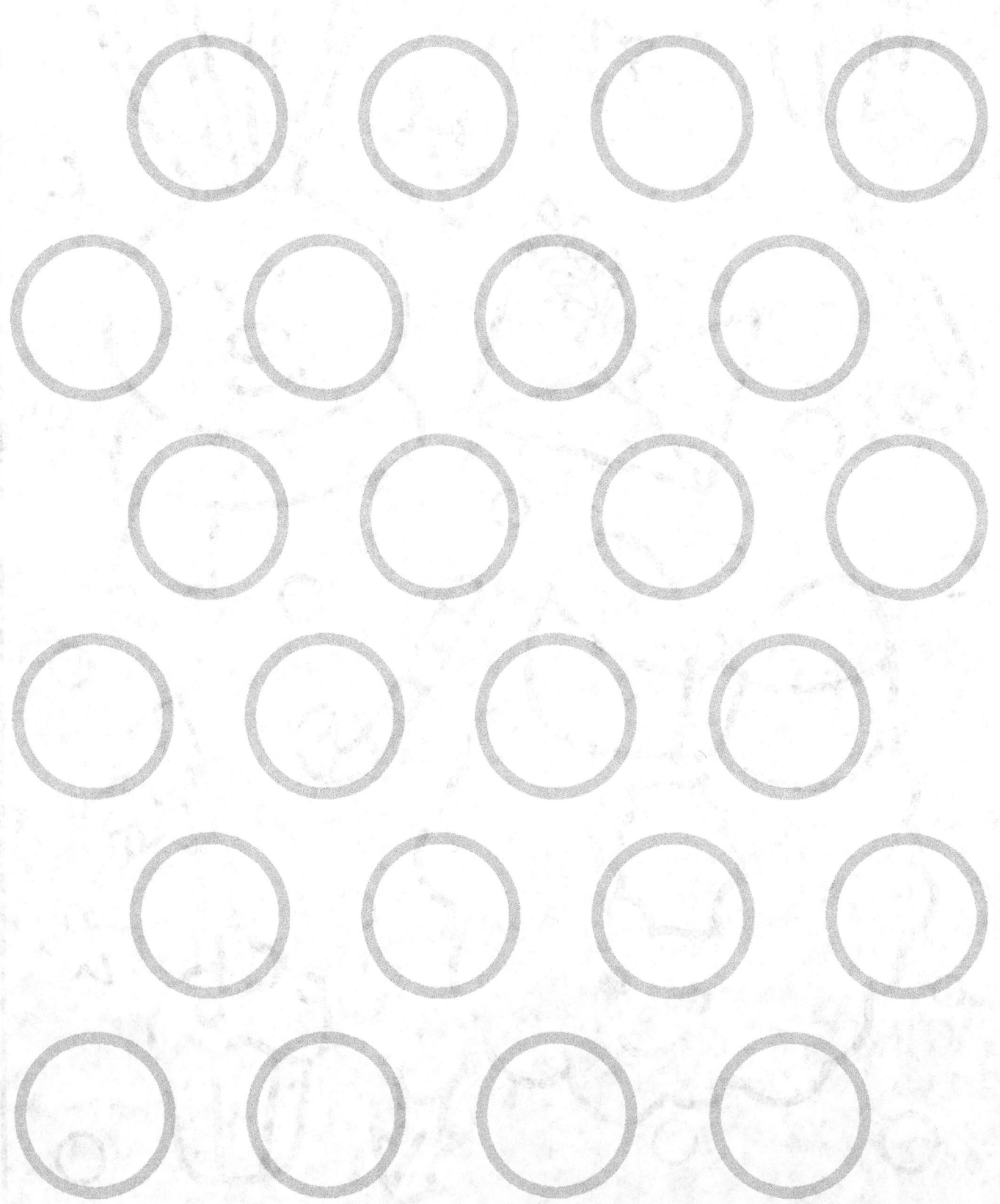